HORSE GAMES & PUZZLES

102 Brainteasers, Word Games, Jokes & Riddles, Picture Puzzles, Matches & Logic Tests for Horse-Loving Kids

Cindy A. Littlefield

Illustrations by Jean Abernethy, Eldon Doty, and Michael Kline

Storey Publishing

The mission of Storey Publishing is to serve our customers by publishing practical information that encourages personal independence in harmony with the environment.

Edited by Deborah Burns
Art direction by Lisa Clark
Cover design by Wendy Palitz
Cover image by www.ronkimball.com
Cover and interior illustrations © Jean Abernethy: front cover (top and bottom), vii, viii, ix, 1, 3, 5, 6, 9, 10, 11, 20, 25, 33, 34, 35, 43, 46, 55, 67, 69, 72, 76, 77, 84, 85, 87, 89, 92, 94 center and bottom, 95 top, 97, 98, 99 bottom, 100, 101, 125; © Eldon Doty: back cover, 2, 7, 14, 23, 29, 31, 37, 44, 45, 47, 48, 49, 52, 53, 56, 57, 59, 60, 61, 63, 71, 74, 75, 78, 79, 86, 90, 94 top, 95 bottom, 96, 99 top; © Michael Kline: front cover (center), iv, v, 19, 26, 50, 51, 54, 58, 62, 64, 65, 70, 72, 73, 88, 91, 93
Text design by Karin Stack
Text production by Melanie Jolicoeur and Doug Bantz

Storey books are available for special premium and promotional uses and for customized editions. For further information, please call 1-800-793-9396.

Printed in the United States by Versa Press
30 29 28 27 26 25 24 23

Library of Congress Cataloging-in-Publication Data

Littlefield, Cindy A., 1956–
    Horse games & puzzles for kids : 102 brainteasers, word games, jokes & riddles, picture puzzles, matches & logic tests for horse-loving kids / Cindy A. Littlefield.
        p. cm.
    Includes bibliographical references and index.
    ISBN 978-1-58017-538-8 (alk. paper)
    1. Horses—Miscellanea—Juvenile literature. 2. Puzzles—Juvenile literature. I. Title.
SF302.L58 2004
793.73—dc22
                                                                                            2004001519

To Kathy, Cheryl, Martha, Robin, Bambi,
John, and all my other riding buddies.

With much gratitude to my great teachers,
especially my 4-H leader, Mrs. Jones, the
instructors at Pony Club, and all my men-
tors from Shannon Trails Riding Stable.

Very special thanks to the horses I had
the pleasure to ride and care for:
Wendy, Silverbird, Shadow, Nizzar,
Shotgun, Lyric, Sassy, and Bid.

CONTENTS

....

Introduction

If you're a kid who's into horses, you probably do or think about something horse-related just about every waking moment. No wonder. There's a lot to love about our equine pals. Spending time riding, caring for, or even simply observing these noble creatures can teach horse fans plenty about being perceptive, patient, responsible, proud, and, not least of all, fun loving!

This book is a celebration of all the fascinating things there are to learn about and from horses, like conformation and equine antics, riding styles and sports, horse lingo, and much more. Chock-full of puzzles, games, brainteasers, and riddles, it will keep you entertained for hours by putting your horse sense to the test and, we hope, providing you with a wealth of new fun facts to share with your fellow horse lovers.

Enjoy the ride!

Word Puzzles

Hungry as a Horse

Hidden in the block of letters is a smorgasbord of horse treats. See if you can find and circle all 14 of them (they are printed in all directions, even diagonally). Some letters are used more than once. When you're done, print the leftover letters, in order, in the spaces below, and you'll find out what else horses need their fill of.

ALFALFA
APPLES
BARLEY
BRAN
CARROTS
CLOVER
CORN
GRASS
HAY
MOLASSES
OATS
PELLETS
SALT
SUGAR

```
M  S  H  A  L  F  A  L  F  A
O  O  T  B  R  S  E  C  S  P
L  N  E  E  A  O  A  T  S  P
A  Y  E  D  L  R  N  P  L  L
S  A  E  N  R  L  L  R  T  E
S  H  Y  O  S  O  E  E  O  S
E  F  T  S  C  V  N  P  Y  C
S  S  A  L  O  R  A  G  U  S
L  R  E  L  A  A  R  N  W  A
G  T  C  E  R  S  B  T  O  O
```

Answer:

_ _ _ _ _ _   _ _ _ _   _ _ _ _ _ _   _ _   _ _ _ _ _   _ _ _ _ _   _ _ _ !

Horse Stages

Below are seven words used to describe horses of different ages and genders. Using a different color pencil or crayon for each word, draw a line connecting the letters you need to spell each word. You can go in any direction. In the end, all of the letters should be drawn through at least once. For an example, the first word is done for you.

~~YEARLING~~, FOAL, COLT, FILLY, MARE, STALLION, GELDING

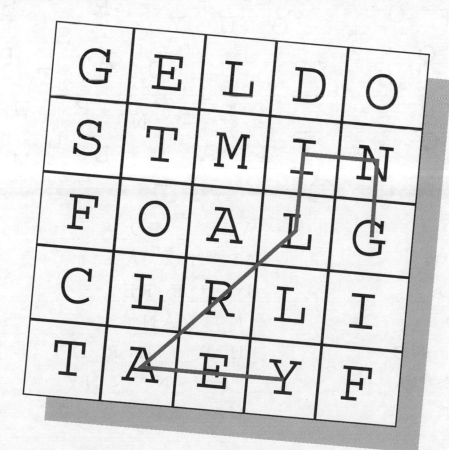

For answers, see page 102

Round Up the Herd

The cowboys at ABC Ranch have asked you to help them gather the herd. It's a very special herd, as each horse or pony is a different breed. To find out which breeds they are, all you have to do is use the letters in the corral to fill in the blanks in the list below it. Cross out the letters as you use them, and it will get easier and easier to round up the next horse.

I A H E S R N D H B E
G E A S T B R Z A P L I
S I T O K O U Y R R A G
D O Q S Y S A P H
D H P T L P O P T D
L B O M F I A N E L W M T E

P _ N _ O   WEL _ _   PO _ _
_ O _ G _ N   AP _ _ L _ _ _ A
AR _ _ IA _   S _ _ D _ E _ RE _
_ JO _ D   _ I _ _ _ ZAN
_ A _ O _ _ NO   _ H _ R _ _ _ H _ R _ D
CL _ _ E _ DA _ _   _ _ E _ L _ N _ _ _ NY
_ A _ NT   _ UA _ _ ER _ O _ _ E

_ _ NN _ SS _ E _ _ L _ IN _ _ OR _ E

For answers, see page 103

Circle Round

I f you pick the right letter to start with and then go around the circle twice stopping on every other letter, you will spell out an interesting fact about the way horses catch up on their sleep.

Fact:

Horse Sightings

Listed below are a dozen locations where you might spot a horse. See if you can fit all of the words into the grid. To get you started, one is already put in place.

STABLE   ARENA
RODEO   RANCH
CORRAL   SHOW
PARADE   TRAIL
PASTURE   STALL
TRAILER   PADDOCK

S T A B L E

Alphabetical Scramble

The 26 words below are meant to name parts of a horse's body, but each one is missing a certain letter. In each case, it is a different letter of the alphabet. See if you can restore the correct letter to each word. For example, the hardest one, the letter *x*, is already done for you. If you add *x* to *coccy*, you create the word *coccyx*, which is the name of a bone in the horse's tail.

a b c d e f g h i j k l m n o p q r s t u v w x̸ y z

tal   hoo
shouler   ri
dok   uarter
mae   bck
cest   erot
chin grooe   fank
aw   gasin
sifle   witers
crou   elbo
patern   chek
muzle   coccy (x↶) = coccyx
pll   forear
ee   chestnt

For answers, see page 104

Categories

Each string of horse-related words shown here belongs in a unique category. To figure out what that category is, all you need to do is unscramble the letters to the right of the group.

Morgan, Thoroughbred, Arabian, Mustang	DREBES
saddle, bridle, martingale, halter, harness	ACTK
stalls, loft, tack room, office	BATESL
corn, pellets, barley, bran	EDESF
snaffle, curb, Pelham, straight	SIBT
cow hocks, parrot mouth, bandy legs, mutton withers	TFEDECS
wolf, incisors, canines	HETET
oxer, vertical, spread, roll top	SPUJM
snip, sock, bald, half-heel	GRINSKAM
ergot, stifle, throatlatch, fetlock	MAYOATN
Haflinger, Hackney, Shetland	SNEIOP
net, electric, wood	IFGENCN

For answers, see page 104

Horse Lovers

The seven clues below describe people who care for and ride horses for a living. Print the answers in the appropriate rows and the name of an eighth horse lover will be spelled out in the shaded column.

1. Someone who cares for sick horses
2. A person who bathes and brushes horses
3. This person raises horses out west
4. Someone who shoes horses
5. An experienced rider
6. A person who races horses
7. Someone who breeds horses

For answers, see page 104

In a Name

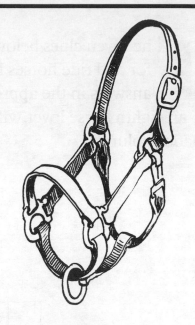

To spruce up his barn, the stable owner decided to have stall door signs painted for the ten horses that were boarded there. He gave the artist a list of the horses' names and descriptions and requested that the lettering be big enough to read from a distance. When the artist dropped off the finished signs, the owner couldn't make heads or tails of them. Instead of lettering the horses' names, the artist had printed the descriptions. Plus, he made the letters so big he could fit only a few on each sign. Can you match up each sign to the horse it was intended for?

SIGN LIST

Mary   the Merry Morgan _____

Adrienne   the Amusing Appaloosa _____

Paul   the Playful Palomino _____

Theodore   the Thoughtful Thoroughbred _____

Connie   the Curious Connemara _____

Shirley   the Sheepish Shetland _____

Priscilla   the Personable Percheron _____

Billy   the Brave Belgian _____

Freddy   the Friendly Fjord _____

Andrew   the Agreeable Arabian _____

For answers, see page 105

1. e n d
   j o r

2. e r s
   h e r

3. a y f
   a l o

4. i o u
   e m a

5. p i s
   e t l

6. h t f
   h b r

7. m e r
   g a n

8. r a v
   g i a

9. s i n
   a l o

10. e a b
    a b i

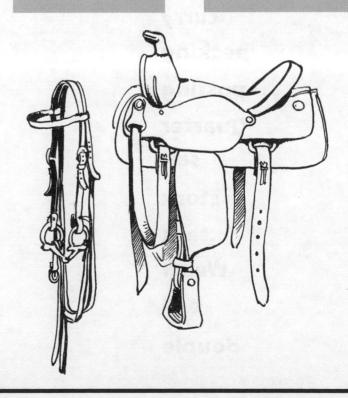

2-in-1 Words

All 36 terms printed below are words in their own right, but draw a line to pair each of them with the correct one in the opposite column, and you'll create 18 new terms that relate to horses.

hoof	seat
horse	bone
saddle	boot
barrel	pad
box	stall
cannon	shoe
barn	order
hay	Horse
curry	Pony
pecking	pick
posting	bale
Quarter	racing
salt	room
stock	bridle
tack	trot
Welsh	block
bell	comb
double	sour

For answers, see page 105

Sidestep

The object here is to spell six words (*bar, frog, quarter, sole, toe,* and *wall*) that name parts of a horse's foot. To do it, you need to slide the individual letters to the right or left on each line so that the correct letters line up vertically. Here's a hint: When lined up correctly, the words will not be in alphabetical order.

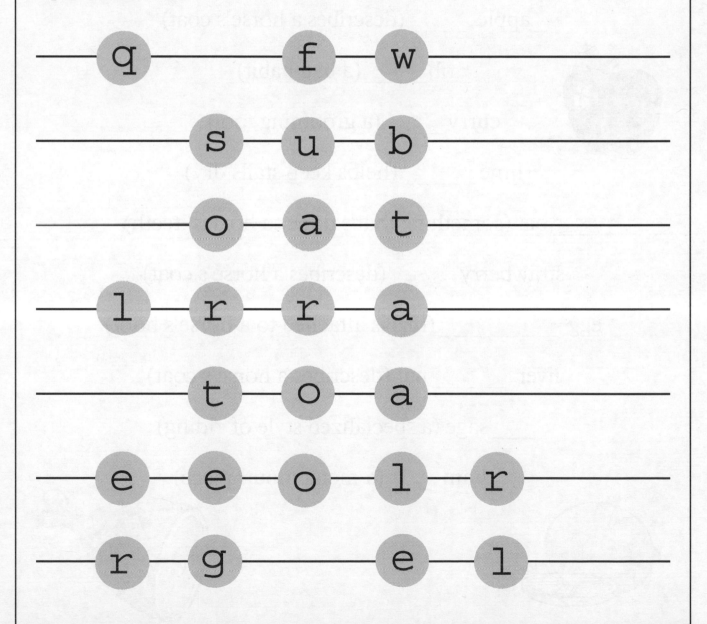

For the answer, see page 105

Food for Thought

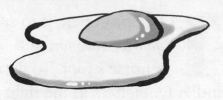

E ach of the food words below is part of a bigger horse-related word or term. See if you can add the right letters to spell the new words using the accompanying clues.

_ _ pizza _ (a breed of horses)

_ apple _ _ _ _ (describes a horse's coat)

_ rib _ _ _ _ (a bad habit)

curry _ _ _ _ (a grooming tool)

lime _ _ _ _ _ (helps keep stalls dry)

_ _ oat (something that's done to horses' teeth)

strawberry _ _ _ _ (describes a horse's coat)

egg - _ _ _ _ _ _ _ (this is attached to a horse's hoof)

liver _ _ _ _ _ nut (describes a horse's coat)

_ _ _ _ sage (a specialized style of riding)

_ _ _ ham _ _ _ (a metal mouthpiece)

For answers, see page 105

Dressing for the Occasion

Tucked away in this word-search puzzle are 20 items (listed at the bottom of the page) that English and Western riders need to outfit themselves from head to toe. See if you can find and circle them all. It may be a little tricky, as the words are printed forward, backward, up, down, and diagonally.

```
S H I R T S T S I S B T
J A C K E T B L M R E E
Y E T V S S V O E E I M
P O O A B Q G E W B T L
T L J O F Y C Z C L S E
G W O A R H F V H N E H
E T D Y E R E L A F F R
S I H S B S E E P E R S
W U P G T R J K S R A T
S R U P S T E K O D C O
D D R O L O B D Z H S C
G Q S N O S T E T S C K
```

BELT	**CHAPS**	**JACKET**	**SPURS**
BOLO	**CHOKER**	**JEANS**	**STETSON**
BOOTS	**DERBY**	**JODHPURS**	**STOCK**
BOWLER	**GLOVES**	**SCARF**	**TIE**
BREECHES	**HELMET**	**SHIRT**	**VEST**

For answers, see page 106

Sugar Cube Sayings

If you reorder the lettered sugar cubes in each row a certain way, you'll end up with a familiar horse phrase or saying.

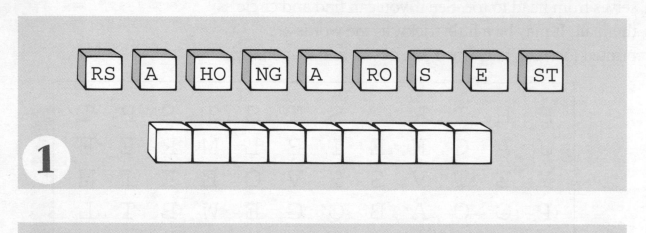

1

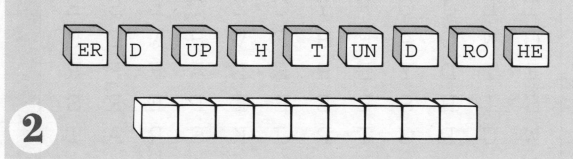

2

3

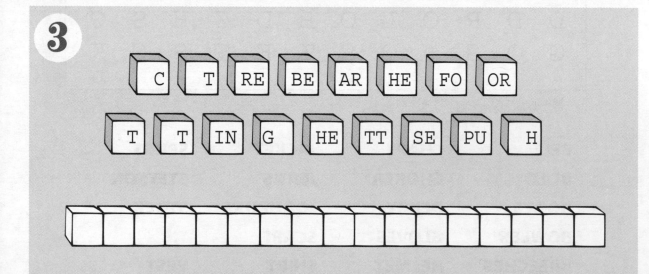

For answers, see page 106

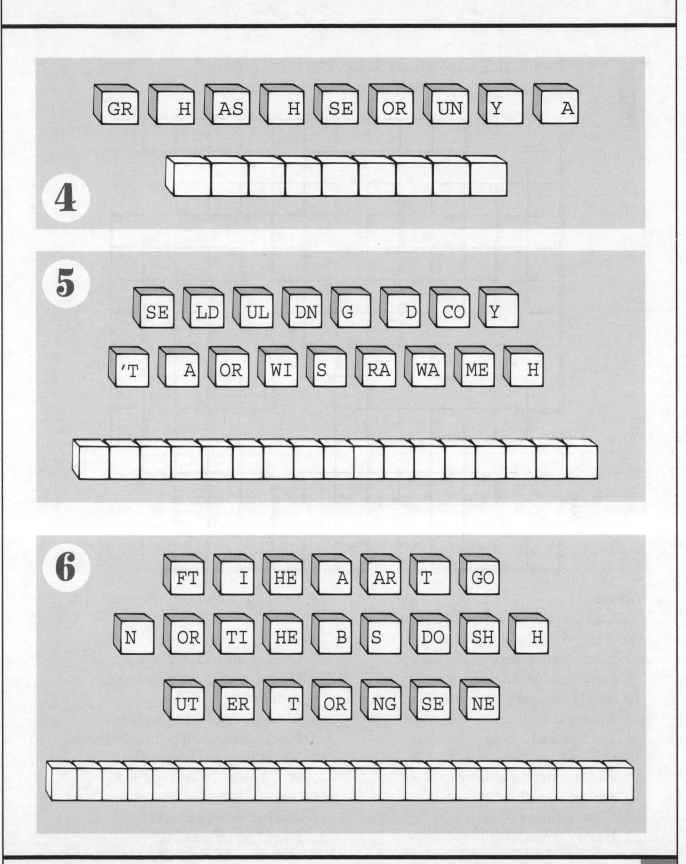

4

GR H AS H SE OR UN Y A

5

SE LD UL DN G D CO Y
'T A OR WI S RA WA ME H

6

FT I HE A AR T GO
N OR TI HE B S DO SH H
UT ER T OR NG SE NE

A Sweep through the Barn

The clues to this crossword puzzle refer to all types of things you're likely to find in and around a stable.

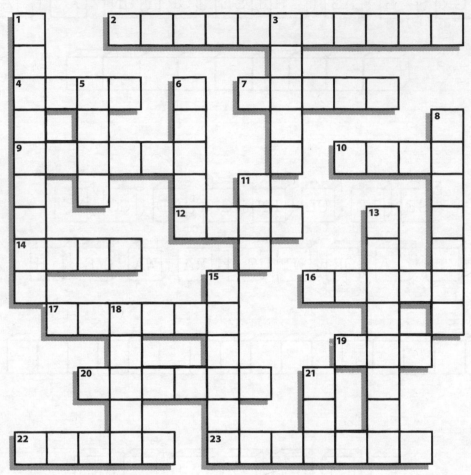

Across

2. Cart you fill when you clean a stall
4. Name for saddle, bridle, etc.
7. Cloth used to wipe down a horse
9. Basic headgear a horse wears
10. Used to spread shavings and smooth dirt
12. Riding aid
14. Used to lead a horse
16. Oats, barley, corn
17. Holds water for a horse to drink
19. Part of a bridle
20. What a rider sits on
22. Has a mane and tail
23. Bedding that's very absorbent

Down

1. Used to lift and throw hay
3. Used to sweep the tack room
5. A male foal
6. Bedding that looks like hay
8. Newspaper, sand, peanut hulls, etc.
11. Something grain is stored in
13. Wood product used for bedding
15. Individual enclosures inside a barn
18. Leather riding apparel
21. Placed under a saddle

For answers, see page 107

Wacky Phrase Craze

If the answers to the clues below
Tend to come a little slow,
Try thinking of two-word phrases that rhyme
And you'll have all the solutions in practically no time.

Here's an example so you can see:
What do you a call a barn with TV?
There is indeed a comic label,
And that would be a cable stable.

❶ young female horse that's very funny
s i l l y _ _ _ _ _

❷ moldy dried grass
g r a y _ _ _

❸ route taken by extremely slow horse
s n a i l _ _ _ _ _

❹ piece of tack that's not in use
i d l e _ _ _ _ _ _

❺ small fake horse
p h o n y _ _ _ _

❻ worn-out saddle blanket
b a d _ _ _

❼ black baby horse
c o a l _ _ _ _

❽ locomotive that's transporting horse feed
_ _ _ _ _ t r a i n

For answers, see page 107

Riding Rings

If you pick the right place to start on each circle and read the letters clockwise in some cases, counterclockwise in others, they will spell a particular style of riding.

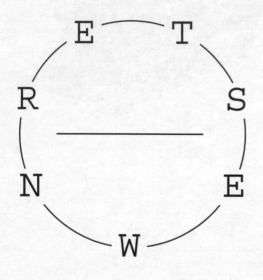

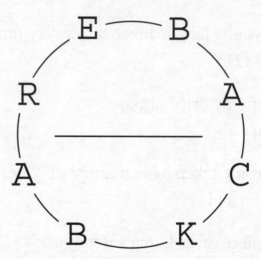

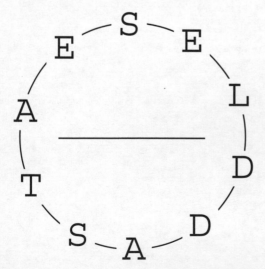

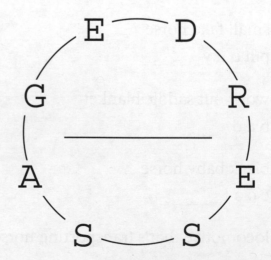

For answers, see page 108

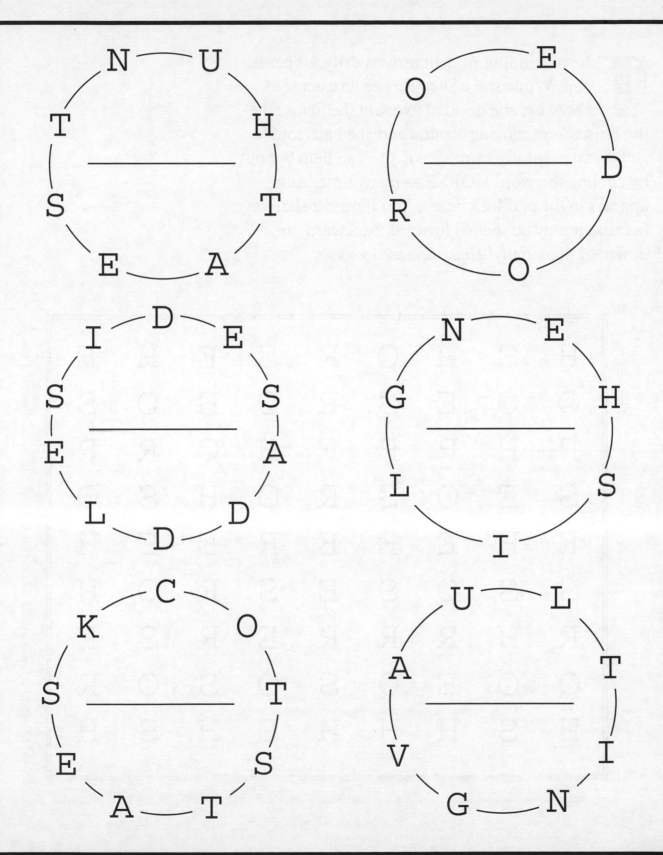

How Many Horses?

The new riding student arrived early for her lesson. While she waited for her instructor to show up, she decided to count the herd, but the horses kept moving around and she had trouble getting an accurate count. See if you can help her out by circling the word HORSE as many times as it appears in the paddock below. You'll need a sharp eye because it may be spelled forward, backward, up, down, or diagonally! *Hint: there are 16 horses.*

```
H  S  H  O  R  S  E  H  E
O  O  E  S  R  O  H  O  S
R  H  R  R  E  H  O  R  R
S  E  O  S  R  O  H  S  O
E  H  E  E  E  R  E  E  H
S  S  O  S  E  S  R  O  H
R  H  R  R  R  E  R  S  E
O  O  E  O  S  O  S  O  R
H  S  H  H  H  E  H  S  H
```

Duos

If you insert the right pair of letters from the box below into each string of letters on the left, you will end up with a list of horse-related words. Here's an example to get you started. **SA LE = SADDLE**

↑

DD

One tip: The puzzle will become easier and easier to solve if you cross out each pair as you place it.

H F

_____

A L E

_____

F I Y

_____

L A O

_____

S T A

_____

P O E L

_____

G A O P

_____

LL	
SS	
OO	
PP	
LL RR	
FF	
LL SS	
MM	
RR LL	
SS	

S N A L E   C A V E O N

_____   _____

F A I E R   H E A D S T A

_____   _____

D R E A G E   C U Y C O M B

_____   _____

Solo Switch

See if you can change just one letter in each of the following words to create a new word that describes part of a horse's conformation.

❶ blank

❷ crust

❸ duck

❹ hoot

❺ loans

❻ mine

❼ nuzzle

❽ peel

❾ rack

❿ tall

For answers, see page 108

Lead or Trail

See if you can answer the following questions by replacing each letter in the solution with the letter that comes immediately before or after it in the alphabet. For example, the letter *B* can be replaced with an *A* or a *C*.

What is a piebald?

B GPQTF SGBU JR

_ _ _ _ _ _ _ _ _ _ _ _

CMBBL BOE XIHUD

_ _ _ _ _ _ _ _ _ _ _ _

What is a skewbald?

B IPSRD UGBS HT XIHUD

_ _ _ _ _ _ _ _ _ _ _ _ _ _ _

BME BOZ PUGDQ DPKNQ

_ _ _ _ _ _ _ _ _ _ _ _ _ _

UIBM CKBBJ

_ _ _ _ _ _ _ _ _

For answers, see page 109

Tack Cubes

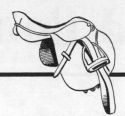

Each of the cubes contains words that relate to a saddle or bridle. To find them, you need to rearrange the letters in each vertical column. For example, the letters in the far left column of the first cube *(nhro)* can be rearranged to spell the word *horn*.

①

n	t	r	o
h	a	n	f
r	s	i	k
o	e	e	r

③

n	n	m	l	e	i
c	d	e	p	p	l
t	f	m	h	e	g
e	e	p	e	k	i
a	r	l	m	r	n
l	e	o	a	e	n

②

a	h	t	r	n
b	k	r	i	i
l	n	g	s	h
s	a	h	t	c
o	s	i	k	c

④

f	k	i	h	w	u	o
s	n	r	e	e	s	b
a	l	p	e	t	b	o
l	b	s	l	n	c	r
f	t	r	t	i	l	n
e	e	t	r	o	k	d
n	a	u	a	d	e	i

For answers, see page 109

Post and Rails

O n each of the fence posts shown here is a horse-related word whose individual letters begin or end another horse-related word. Using the clues provided, see how many new words you can come up with to fill in the empty rails.

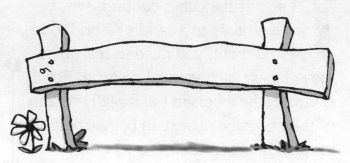

type of riding whip ☐☐☐ **P**

A ☐☐☐☐☐ kind of hay

goes under the saddle ☐☐ **D**

D ☐☐☐☐☐ fancy style of riding

rope used in Western riding ☐☐☐☐ **O**

C ☐☐☐☐ a gait

part of the tail ☐☐☐ **K**

F ☐☐☐ part of the hoof

enclosure where competitive
Western events are held ☐☐☐☐☐ **A**

R ☐☐☐ includes bronc riding
and calf roping

an especially tasty hay ☐☐☐☐ **R**

I ☐☐☐ English term for stirrups

facial marking ☐☐☐☐ **E**

R ☐☐☐☐ to shave a mane

For answers, see page 109

Puzzle 1 (across TROT):

band above the hoof _ _ _ _ _ _

awarded to horse show riders _ _ _ _ _ _

game played on horseback _ _ _

bridles, saddles, and other gear _ _ _ _

Puzzle 2 (across STABLE):

might come with a horn _ _ _ _ _

part of a bridle _ _

crunchy treat _ _ _ _

horse that is slightly larger than a pony _ _

right or left, depending on which leg strikes the ground first _ _ _ _

sometimes braided _ _ _ _

Puzzle 3 (across HORSEMANSHIP):

what you clip a lead line to _ _ _ _ _

has large splotches of white and another color _ _ _ _ _

coat coloring that looks speckled _ _ _ _

attached to the bit _ _ _ _

horny part behind the fetlock _ _ _ _

brushes and cares for horses _ _ _ _ _

breed with a dished face and an arched neck _ _ _ _ _

American breed known for its strength _ _ _ _ _

boxlike enclosure in a barn _ _ _ _

also called a girth _ _ _ _

hardy horse breed _ _ _ _ _ _ _ _

for a rider's foot _ _ _ _ _ _

Shadow Boxes

I f you match each item in Column A with the proper grid in Column B, the letters in the unshaded boxes will spell a word that relates to the key subject.

B T O C X B E K S → ⬜B⬜ ▨T▨ ⬜O⬜ ▨C▨ ▨X▨ ▨B▨ ⬜E⬜ ▨K▨ ⬜S⬜ = B ▨▨ O X ▨▨ E S

Column A   **Column B**

Feeds

B P R A G N

C S O R N L

D O A B T S

Column A   **Column B**

Gaits

M K L B O T P E

P O A C A U N E

T R J F O Y T B

J W Q A L V K Z

G I A L F L O P

Column A   **Column B**

Tack

F H A R L X T E E R

H T A R N B E S S H

T S P A D T D W L E

B C L R I D O L E T

Sounds Just Like...

Each of the words listed below has a horse homonym, a word that sounds exactly the same but is spelled differently and means something different. Can you guess what they are?

And for the grand-prize question: Name a horse word that sounds just like *hoarse*.

horse?

Welcome to
The Horsing Around GAME SHOW

hawk   _ _ _ _

main   _ _ _ _

tale   _ _ _ _

heard   _ _ _ _

gate   _ _ _ _

pole   _ _ _ _

hey   _ _ _

Strike Out

It takes only a few strokes of your pencil to turn the words on the left into words that describe horses. The column in the middle tells you how many letters to cross out in each case.

Original Word	Number of Letters to Cross Out	Horse-related Word
collect	3	_ _ _ _
football	4	_ _ _ _
finally	2	_ _ _ _ _
study	1	_ _ _ _
marble	2	_ _ _ _

For answers, see page 110

Get a Clue!

Each of the grids shown here can be filled with a certain word that pertains to horses or horseback riding. To help you figure out what those words are, you'll find a couple of clues to shorter words that are spelled using letters that also belong in the grid. As an example, the first clue below grid A has already been solved for you.

			o	m		n	o
①	②	③	④	⑤	⑥	⑦	⑧

A **Letters**   **Spell a word that:**

5,4,8,7   lights the barnyard at night = moon

1,2,6,3   a horse can drink water from this

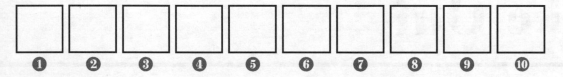

①	②	③	④	⑤	⑥	⑦	⑧	⑨	⑩

B **Letters**   **Spell a word that:**

7,1,8,10   describes an item in your hand when riding

5,8,7,4   identifies a horse's father

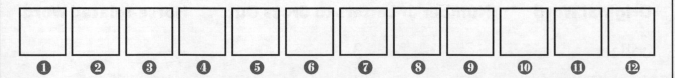

①	②	③	④	⑤	⑥	⑦	⑧	⑨	⑩	⑪	⑫

C **Letters**   **Spell a word that:**

4,2,11,9   is another term to describe a horse's hoof

1,8,6,9   describes something a horse or pony might pull

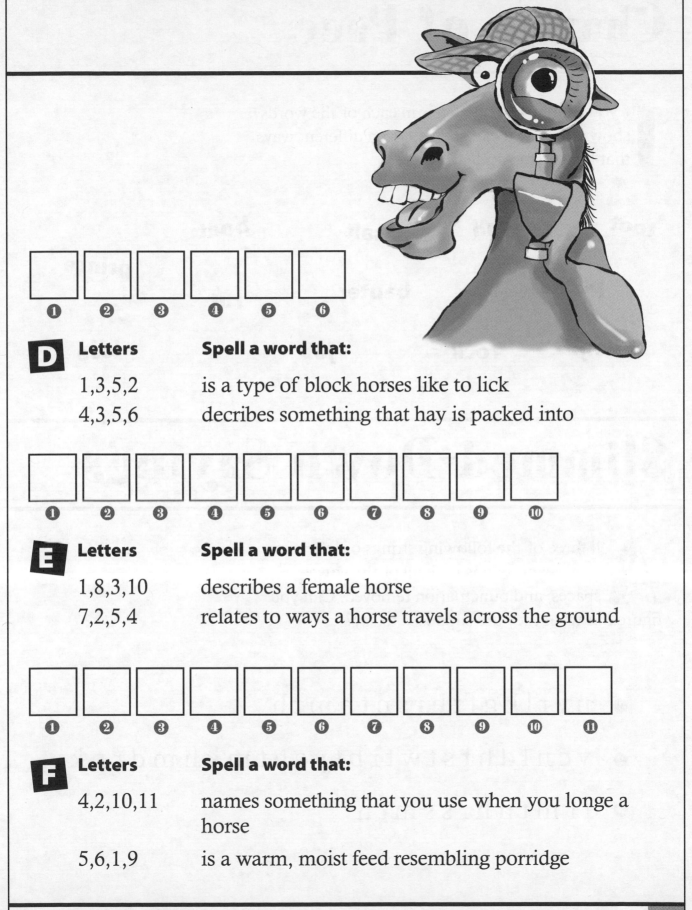

①	②	③	④	⑤	⑥

D **Letters** **Spell a word that:**

1,3,5,2 is a type of block horses like to lick

4,3,5,6 decribes something that hay is packed into

①	②	③	④	⑤	⑥	⑦	⑧	⑨	⑩

E **Letters** **Spell a word that:**

1,8,3,10 describes a female horse

7,2,5,4 relates to ways a horse travels across the ground

①	②	③	④	⑤	⑥	⑦	⑧	⑨	⑩	⑪

F **Letters** **Spell a word that:**

4,2,10,11 names something that you use when you longe a horse

5,6,1,9 is a warm, moist feed resembling porridge

For answers, see page 110

Change of Pace

If you change just one letter in each of the words shown here, you can spell a dozen different ways that horses stop and go.

toot wall salt boat

pack banter rut prince

pump rock job lose

Slimmed-Down Sayings

All three of the following strings of letters are horse expressions with all of the vowels, spaces, and punctuation removed. Can you figure out what they are supposed to say?

1. n v r l k g f t h r s n t h m t h
2. y c n l d h r s t w t r b t y c n t m k h m d r n k
3. f r m t h h r s s m t h

For answers, see page 111

Horsing Around

The answers to this crossword puzzle describe different kinds of things a horse may do on any given day.

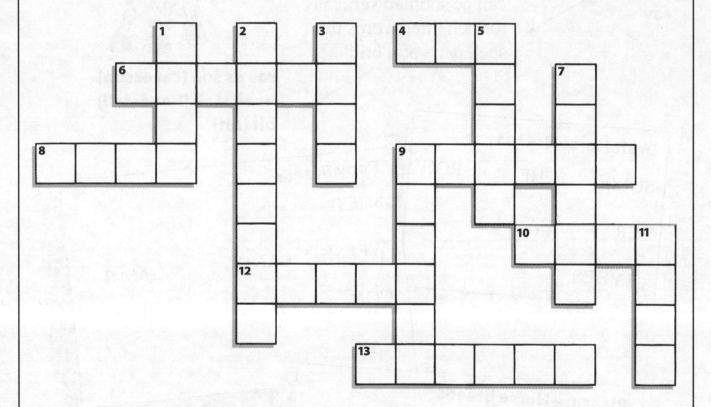

Across

4 A Western word for a slow trot
6 An English term for a smooth 3-beat gait
8 When a horse kicks with both hind legs at the same time
9 Something a horse does with its nose
10 A way that a horse scratches its back after you take off its saddle
12 What horses do at the trough
13 A springy, showy gait

Down

1 A slow 4-beat gait
2 When a herd of horses run wildly
3 A gait that English riders post to
5 What horses do that are put out to pasture
7 A horse's fastest gait
9 A soft noise horses make
11 A Western term for canter

For answers, see page 111

Syllable Shuffle

In the boxes shown here, if you correctly rearrange the syllables in the columns, each row across will spell a word that falls into the identified category. Here's an example to get you started:

**bit stall son
head es
cav**

can be shuffled vertically to spell three words that spell parts of a bridle

**cav es son (cavesson)
head stall (headstall)
bit (bit)**

Draft Horse Breeds

SHIRE   CHE   RON

PER   DALE

CLYDES

Pony Breeds

SHET   NE   GER   A

WELSH   LAND   MAR

CON   LIN

HAF

Pleasure Horse Breeds

MUS   DLE   BI   AN

A   TANG   BRED

PAINT   RA

SAD

For answers, see page 111

Types of Feeds

BRAN   LEY   SES

BAR   LAS

MO

Kinds of Grasses

RYE   VER   THY

CLO   O

TIM

Keeps a Horse Happy and Healthy

EX   TER   ION   LA   TION

IN   ER   CISE   SHIP

REST   PAN   U

COM   OC

SHEL

Equine Ailments

SPLINTS HALT   TI   TIS   TIS

                             VI
STRING   TU   LA

FIS   I   NI

LAM   JUNC

CON

For answers, see page 111

Horseshoe Clues

See how long it takes you to put together the names of the bridle and saddle parts that go below. Here's a hint: The horseshoes that are upside down should be replaced with consonants, while those that are right-side up are place holders for vowels.

= consonant

= vowel

Parts of a BRIDLE

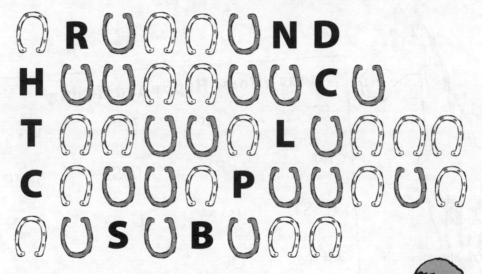

R ⋃ ⋂ ⋂ ⋃ N D
H ⋃ ⋃ ⋂ ⋃ ⋃ C ⋃
T ⋂ ⋂ ⋂ ⋂ L ⋃ ⋂ ⋂ ⋂
C ⋂ ⋂ ⋂ ⋂ P ⋃ ⋂ ⋂ ⋂
⋂ S ⋃ B ⋃ ⋂

Parts of a SADDLE

⋃ ⋃ ⋃ T
G ⋃ ⋂ T ⋂
⋂ G ⋃ M M ⋃ ⋂
C ⋃ ⋂ ⋂ L ⋃
⋂ T ⋃ ⋂ ⋂ ⋃ ⋂ S
F ⋃ ⋂ ⋂
⋂ ⋃ R ⋂

For answers, see page 112

Another Name

Disguised in each word or phrase below is a familiar horse-related term. The key to revealing its identity is to use synonyms — that is, words that have the same or nearly the same meanings as the ones you see.

For example, take the clue **cushionpier**. A synonym for **cushion** is **pad,** and a synonym for **pier** is **dock.** Put the two together and you get **paddock.**

1. SQUARE BOOTH _____

2. OCEANSCONE _____

3. COOL AIR CURRENT EQUINE _____

4. STRIKING SEQUENCE _____

5. CIRCLE DISTASTEFUL _____

6. PERSPIRATION REMOVER _____

7. SODIUM CHUNK _____

8. BARN CUT _____

9. EXHIBITPERSONBOAT _____

For answers, see page 112

What's the Deal?

The horse words and terms printed in the circle below are all shuffled up, but they really belong in four general categories. Can you figure out how to deal them into the proper groups and then label the categories? Need a hint? There's a clue printed upside down at the bottom of the page.

shavings
horseshoe
cavesson
lead chain
saddle
grip reins
cavelletti
rasp
quirt
bit guard
barn
stirrup pads
fence post
stall mats
paddock gate
riding boots
electric fence
sawdust
harness
curb
currycomb
bell boots
shank
show halter

Category:
1
2
3
4
5
6

Category:
1
2
3
4
5
6

Category:
1
2
3
4
5
6

Category:
1
2
3
4
5
6

Hint: Think about what each item is made from.

For answers, see page 112

Color Codes

Printed in each bubble is a term for or description of an item that is horse related. To complete this puzzle, you must draw a line connecting each bubble to the color it is commonly associated with. Keep in mind that some of the bubbles may relate to more than one color.

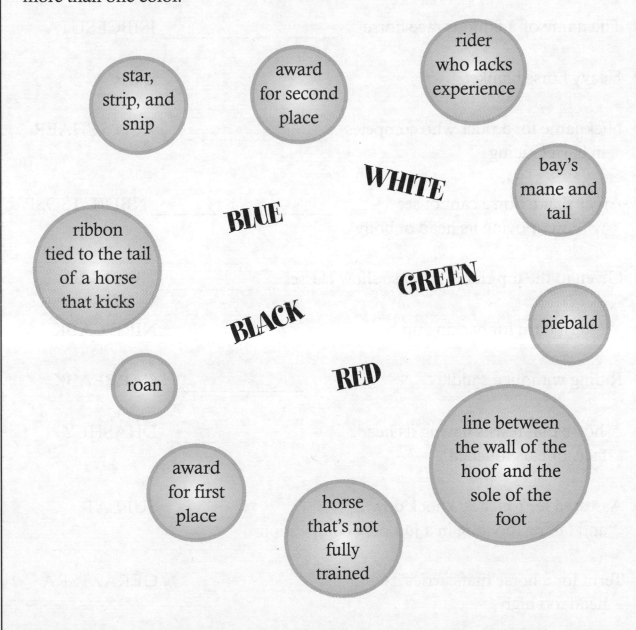

star, strip, and snip

award for second place

rider who lacks experience

bay's mane and tail

WHITE

BLUE

GREEN

ribbon tied to the tail of a horse that kicks

BLACK

piebald

RED

roan

line between the wall of the hoof and the sole of the foot

award for first place

horse that's not fully trained

For answers, see page 113

Scrambled Solutions

The answers to the ten clues listed below are right in front of your eyes, although you may not recognize them, because the letters are all mixed up! See if you can unscramble the solutions and make the matches.

❶ The name of a famous race horse   _ _ _ _ _ _ _ _ _   ISIBCESUTA

❷ Heavy horse blanket   _ _ _   UGR

❸ Nickname for a rider who competes   _ _ _   _ _ _ _ _ _   ACN SCHAER
   in barrel racing

❹ Areas that a horse cannot see   _ _ _ _ _ _   _ _ _ _ _ _   NBDIL TSOSP
   without moving its head or body

❺ Given to the top riders in horse show classes   _ _ _ _ _ _ _   BRSNIBO

❻ Western term for backing up   _ _ _ _   _ _ _ _   NIRE CABK

❼ Riding without a saddle   _ _ _ _ _ _ _ _   CARBEABK

❽ A horse that resists having its head,   _ _ _ _ _ _ _   DHASHEY
   face, or ears touched

❾ Assessed for touches, knock downs,   _ _ _ _ _ _   SUFLAT
   and taking too long in a jumping competition

❿ Term for a horse that carries its   _ _ _ _ _ _ _ _ _   GERAZTSRA
   head too high

By the Numbers

In the horse world, specific numbers often come into play. See if you can transfer the proper numerals from the outer frame into the equations in the inner frame.

Outer frame numbers (clockwise from top): 12, 1,500, 24, 2, 100.5, 4, 8, 3, 4, 10, 2,200, 24, 14.2, 66, 4, 3, 10

gallop = ___ beats

pen = ___ by ___ feet

hand = ___ inches

a healthy horse = ___ to ___ degrees F

event = ___ riding disciplines

walk = ___ beats

draft horse = ___ to ___ pounds

lead rope = ___ to ___ feet

canter = ___ beats

box stall = ___ by ___ feet

pony = ___ or less hands

trot = ___ beats

For answers, see page 113

Desirable Traits

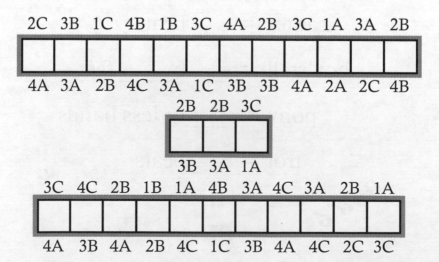

It's important for a rider to consider a couple of general characteristics when choosing a horse. To find out what they are, use the letters in the grid to fill in the empty blocks below it. Printed above and below each of the blocks are coordinates to two possible letters. If you choose the right one in each case, you'll solve the puzzle.

	A	B	C
1	d	p	r
2	i	n	c
3	o	a	t
4	m	f	e

2C 3B 1C 4B 1B 3C 4A 2B 3C 1A 3A 2B

4A 3A 2B 4C 3A 1C 3B 3B 4A 2A 2C 4B

2B 2B 3C

3B 3A 1A

3C 4C 2B 1B 1A 4B 3A 4C 3A 2B 1A

4A 3B 4A 2B 4C 1C 3B 4A 4C 2C 3C

For the answer, see page 113

Picture Puzzlers

Picture Words

The following puzzles, called rebuses, string together pictures, letters, and symbols to represent words and phrases. They're easier to figure out if you say the clues aloud. Try them and see how many you can solve.

1. [horse] + [fly] = _ _ _ _ _ _ _ _

2. [horse] + [shoe] = _ _ _ _ _ _ _

3. [saw] + [horse] = _ _ _ _ _ _ _

4. [horse] + [radish] = _ _ _ _ _ _ _ _ _

5. [horse] + [man] + [ship] = _ _ _ _ _ _ _ _ _ _

Double Talk

Each of the horse-related pictures below shares a name with another item on the page. See if you can match them correctly by drawing a line between each pair.

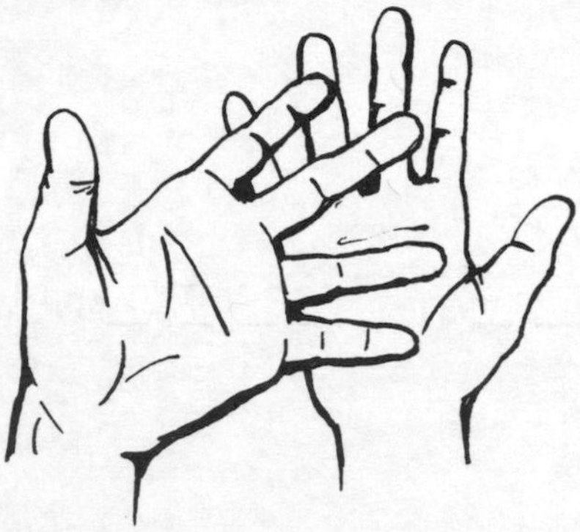

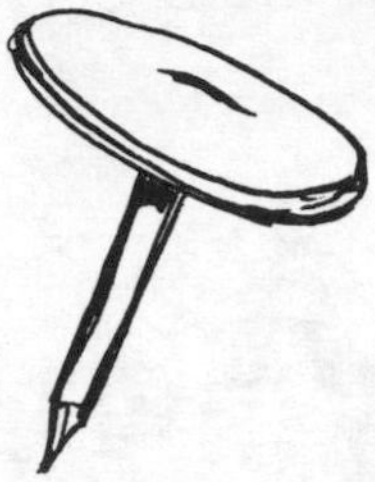

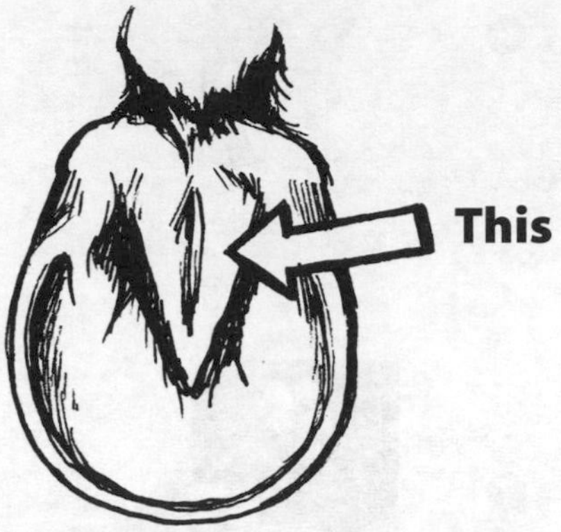

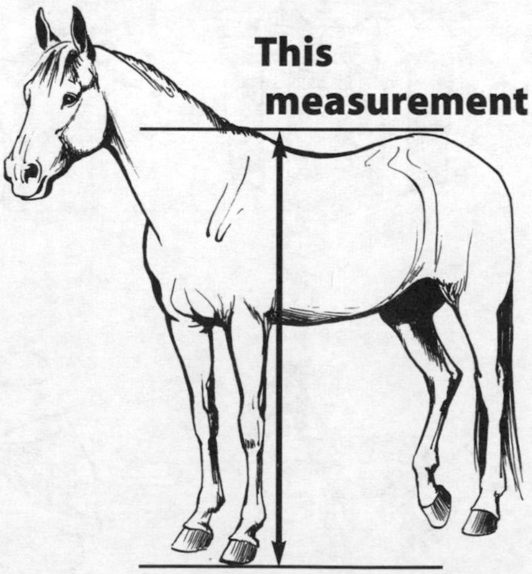

This

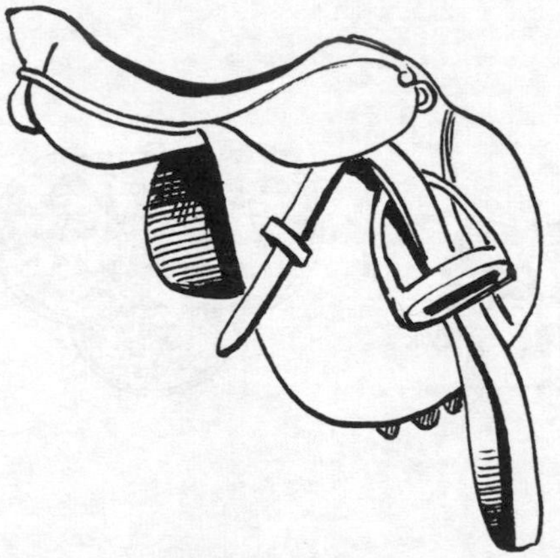

This
measurement

Curry
Powder

For answers, see page 114

Follow the Picture Path

Every morning, the old gray gelding is led from his barn out to pasture following a path of adjacent squares that contain the same item: either a carrot, a horseshoe, a boot, an apple, a pail of water, or a riding helmet. At dinnertime, he's led back to his stall by way of a second path that once again connects adjacent squares that contain a different item. See if you can find those two paths that lead to and from the pasture.

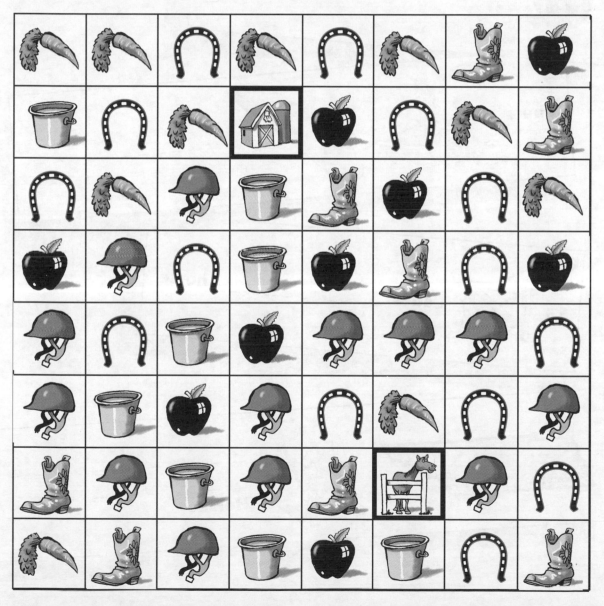

For answers, see page 114

Are You My Type?

Horses are often referred to by their breed, their coloring, or even a specific physical trait. See if you can identify which group each of these word puzzles represents.

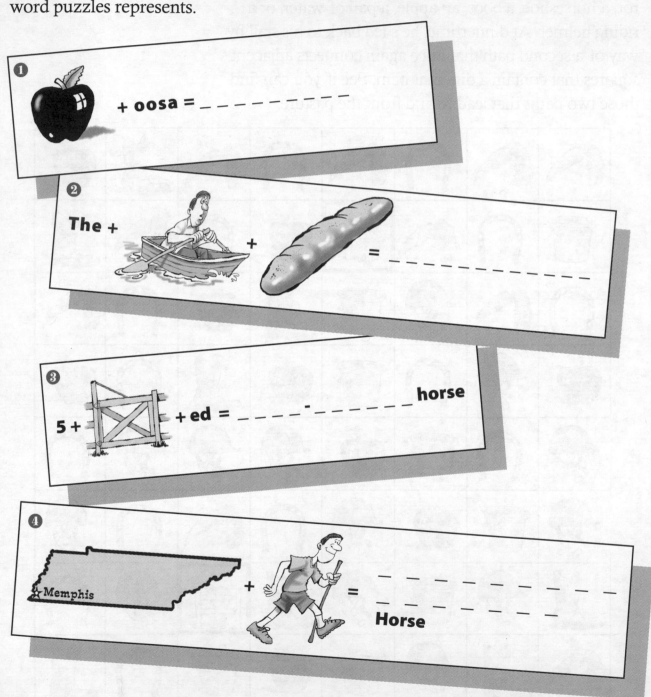

❶ [apple] + oosa = _ _ _ _ _ _ _ _

❷ The + [man rowing boat] + [loaf of bread] = _ _ _ _ _ _ _ _ _ _ _ _

❸ 5 + [gate] + ed = _ _ _ _ - _ _ _ _ horse

❹ [Tennessee map with ★Memphis] + [man walking with rake] = _ _ _ _ _ _ _ _ _ _ _ _ _ Horse

5 + ic = _ _ _ _ _ _ _ _

6 = _ _ _ _ _ **Horse**

7 = _ _ _ _ _

8 = _ _ _ _ _ _ _ **Horse**

9 + skin = _ _ _ _ _ _ _ _

10 + = _ _ _ _ _ _ _ _

For answers, see page 114

Picture Pairs

If each of the pictures shown below is paired with a certain picture on the facing page, it will form a clue to a term that has something to do with horses. See how many clues you can put together and solve by writing the correct number in the blank.

③

①

②

⑥

④

⑤

⑦

⑧

⑨

⑩

For answers, see page 115

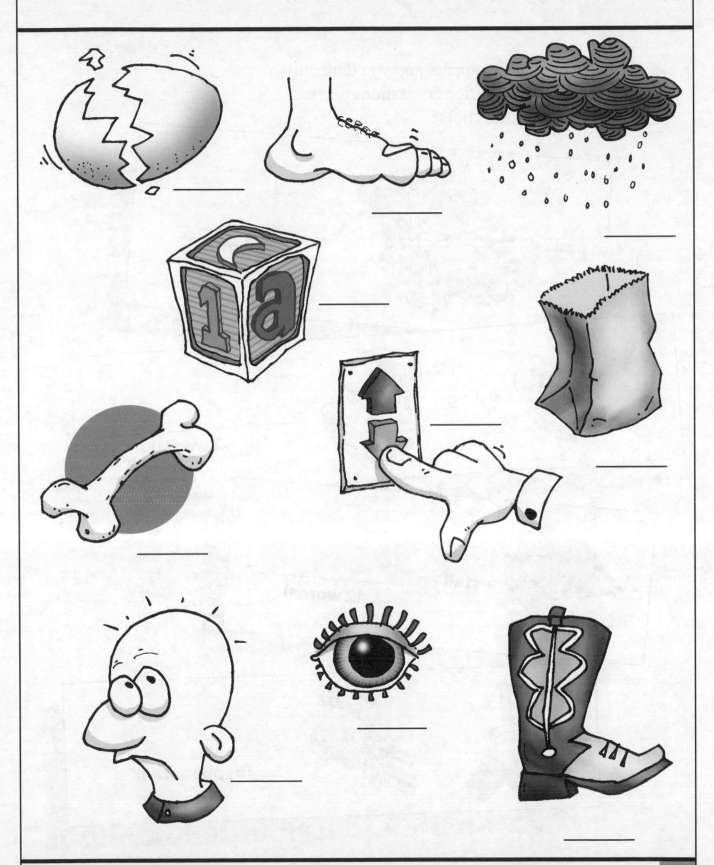

Places & Spaces

Solve these picture puzzles and you'll identify eight common locations or stations where you're apt to find a horse.

1

pad + 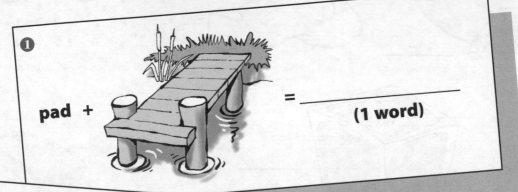 = _____ **(1 word)**

2

r +  + ding = _____ **(2 words)**

3

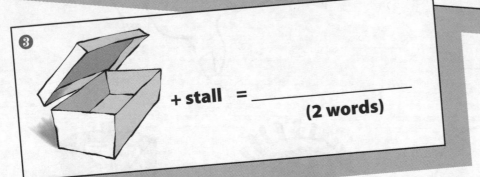 + stall = _____ **(2 words)**

4

 + = _____ **(hyphenated)**

For answers, see page 115

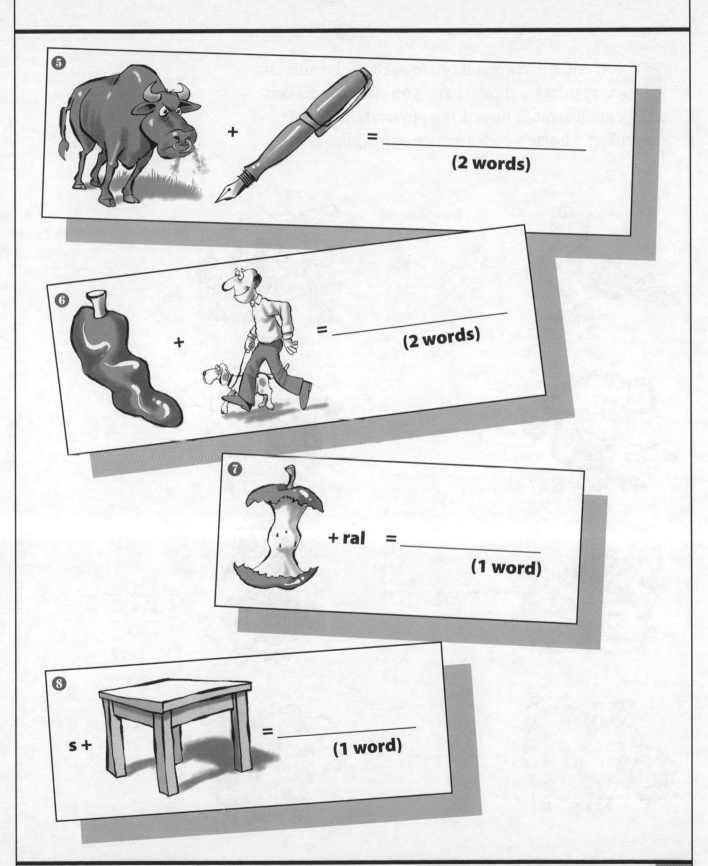

5 + = _____ **(2 words)**

6 + = _____ **(2 words)**

7 + ral = _____ **(1 word)**

8 s + = _____ **(1 word)**

Animal Menagerie

I f you add the correct word to each of the animal picture puzzles shown here, you will name a conformation fault, one of the physical traits that may affect a horse's performance or health.

For answers, see page 115

Horse Sense

The key to solving these five puzzles is to think about the specific items in each box as well as how or where they are pictured.

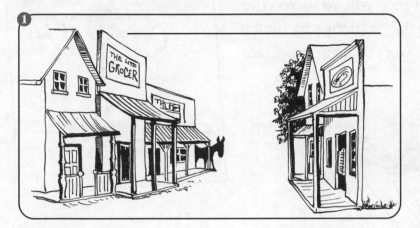

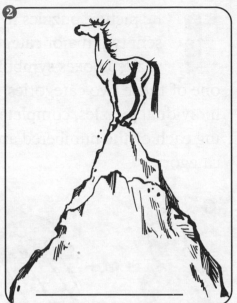

For answers, see page 116

Tack Up!

The picture puzzles in the white boxes represent two major categories of tack; those in the shaded boxes symbolize items that belong in one of those two categories. Once you've solved the individual puzzles, complete the challenge by matching each of the numbered answers to its appropriate category.

+ L

_ _ _ _ _ _ _ _

1
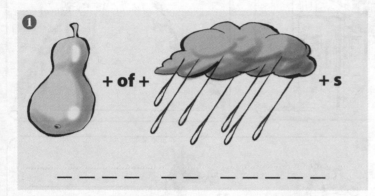

+ of + + s

_ _ _ _ _   _ _   _ _ _ _ _

2

+

_ _ _ _ _ _ _ _

3

½   snaf + L

_ _ _ _ _ - _ _ _ _ _   _ _ _ _ _ _

4

_ _ _ _

5

Pel +
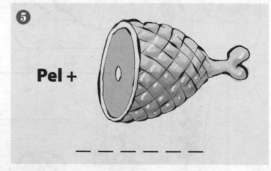

_ _ _ _ _ _

For answers, see page 116

+ **L**

_ _ _ _ _ _ _

⑨

_ _ _ _ _

⑥

+ **tle**

_ _ _ _ _ _ _

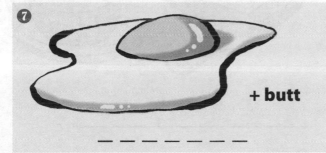

⑦

+ **butt**

_ _ _ _ _ _ _ _

⑩

_ _ _ _ _ _

⑧

+

_ _ _ _ _ _ _ _

For answers, see page 116

Poisonous Plants

S ome plants, though they may be pretty to look at or have fun-sounding names, can make a horse quite sick. Here are clues to a few you may have heard of. How many can you identify?

①

+ bane

④

+

②

+

⑤

+

③

+ neck

⑥

White +

In a Word

The nine words that describe what's in the pictures below are also used to name something to do with horses. See how many of those words and their equine definitions you can come up with.

Motion Pictures

The solutions to these eight puzzles describe assorted sights and sounds associated with a horse in motion.

 + age = _____ (1 word)

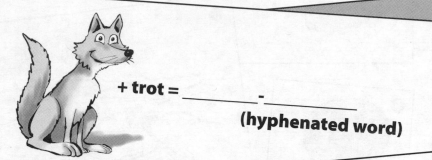 + trot = _____-_____ (hyphenated word)

 + ter = _____ (1 word)

side +  = _____ (1 word)

For answers, see page 117

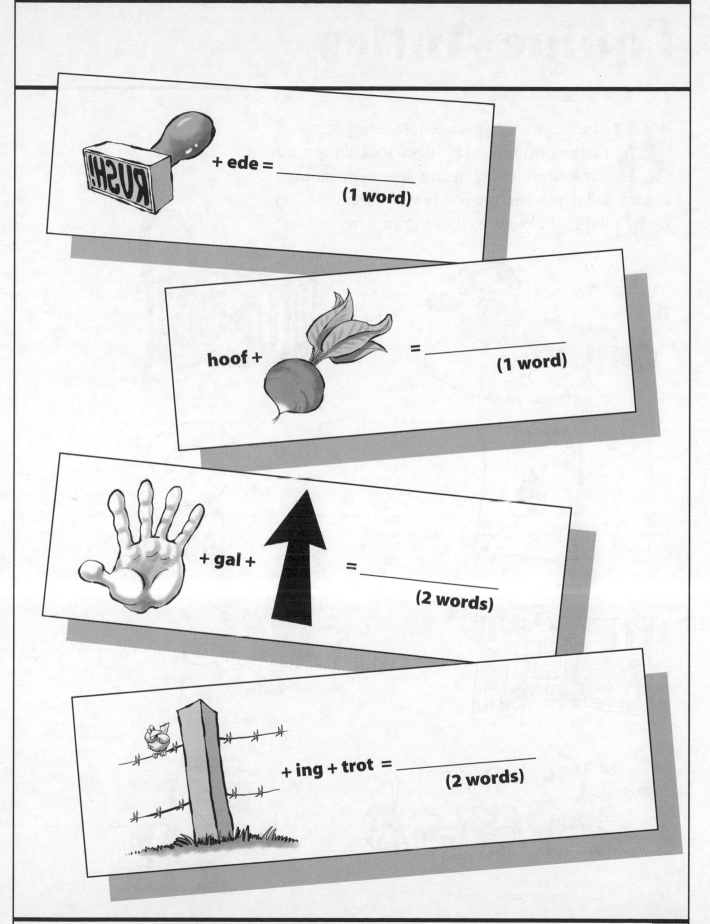

_____ + ede = _____ **(1 word)**

hoof + 🥬 = _____ **(1 word)**

_____ + gal + ⬆ = _____ **(2 words)**

_____ + ing + trot = _____ **(2 words)**

For answers, see page 117

PICTURE PUZZLERS   61

Equine Antics

Horses certainly do some interesting things, ranging from playing tricks, to making amusing sounds, to acting out downright strange habits. See if you can name a few of the things they do by solving the picture clues shown here.

❶ _ _ _ _

❷ _ _ _ _

❸ r + _ _ _ _ _

❹ r + _ _ _ _ _

❺ _ _ _ _ _

❻ + e _ _ _ _ _ _

❼ pr + _ _ _ _ _ _ _

❽ j + _ _ _ _ _

For answers, see page 117

Rhyme Time

The object here is to identify the word that describes each picture and then come up with a horse-related word that rhymes with it. For example, a horse word that rhymes with 🍎 is *dapple*.

For answers, see page 117

Picture Spelling Bee

Each of the pictures shown here is represented by a word that can be spelled using some of the letters found in one of the three featured horse words. See if you can correctly list all of the picture labels under the right horse terms. One is already done for you.

broodmare

1 _ _ _ _ _
2 _ _ _ _
3 _ _ _ _ _
4 _ _ _ _
5 _ _ _

gelding

1 <u>e</u> g g
2 _ _ _ _ _
3 _ _ _ _
4 _ _ _ _ _ _
5 _ _ _

stallion

1 _ _ _ _
2 _ _ _ _ _
3 _ _ _ _ _
4 _ _ _ _
5 _ _ _ _

Box Stalls

The four box stalls below are filled with all kinds of things you might find in and around a horse barn. Although each of the items appears more than once, only three of them can be found in all four stalls. Can you figure out which they are and circle them?

For answers, see page 118

Fun and Games

Symbol Squares

The object here is to draw the right symbol (an apple, a bit, a carrot, a helmet, a hoof pick, a horseshoe, or a sugar cube) in each of the empty boxes in the grid so that each symbol appears only once in each row or column.

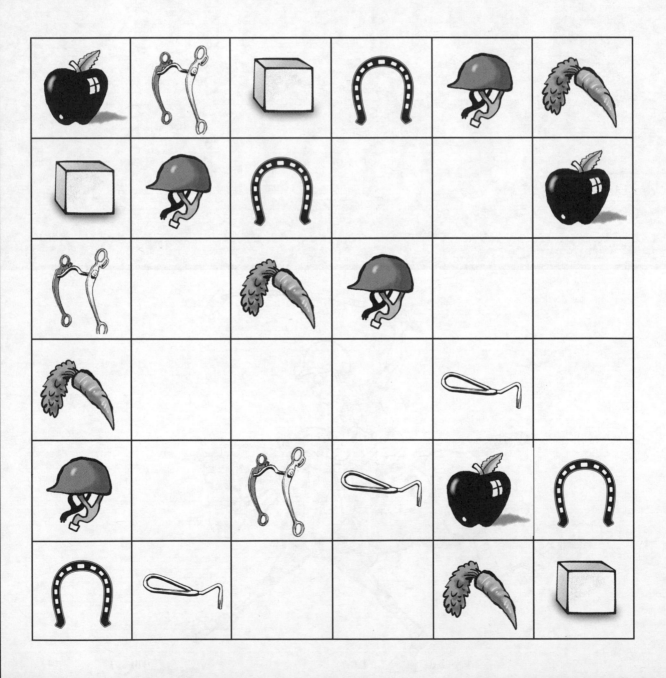

For answers, see page 118

Body Building

L isted here are three dozen horse conformation terms. How many of them can you place next to the appropriate body part?

back	ear	heel	poll
cannon bone	elbow	hock	sheath
cheek	ergot	hoof	shoulder
chestnut	fetlock	jowl	stifle
coronet	flank	knee	tail
coupling	forearm	loin	thigh
crest	forelock	mane	throatlatch
croup	gaskin	muzzle	underline
dock	heart girth	pastern	withers

For answers, see page 118

Cooking Up Horse Names

Besides cooking, the Cantering Chef's favorite pasttime is riding horses. So for his birthday, his family decided to give him a half-dozen horses, each one a different color. Delighted, the cook decided to name the horses after some of his favorite foods. See if you can make the right matches.

Strawberry Roan	**Butterscotch**
Paint	**Shortcake**
Brown	**Powdered Sugar**
Palomino	**Marble Cake**
Black	**Licorice**
Appaloosa	**Cocoa**

For answers, see page 118

Equine Stall of Fame

Can you fill in the correct letter to match up the famous horses and ponies on the left with their human, television character, or celestial companions?

Silver ___

Brown Beauty ___

Mr. Ed ___

The Pie ___

Duke ___

Trigger ___

Buckshot ___

Poky ___

Target ___

Pegasus ___

Phantom ___

Buttermilk ___

Scout ___

A Wild Bill Hickock

B John Wayne

C Gumby

D Zorro

E Annie Oakley

F Paul Revere

G Velvet Brown

H The Lone Ranger

I Dale Evans

J Tonto

K Perseus

L Wilbur Post

M Roy Rogers

For answers, see page 119

Stadium Jumping

Y ou're the last rider in the class and your number's been called. Every other contestant has had at least one fault. If you clear all five jumps (all you have to do is label them correctly), you'll go home with the blue!

5 _____

Clue: This jump, which resembles a little hill, is usually intimidating to horses.

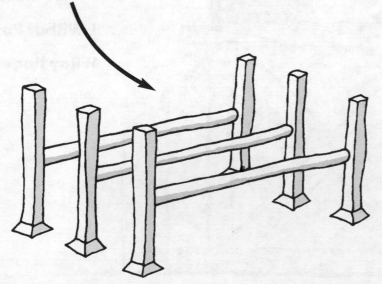

1 _____

Clue: A horse must jump long to clear this extra deep hurdle.

For answers, see page 119

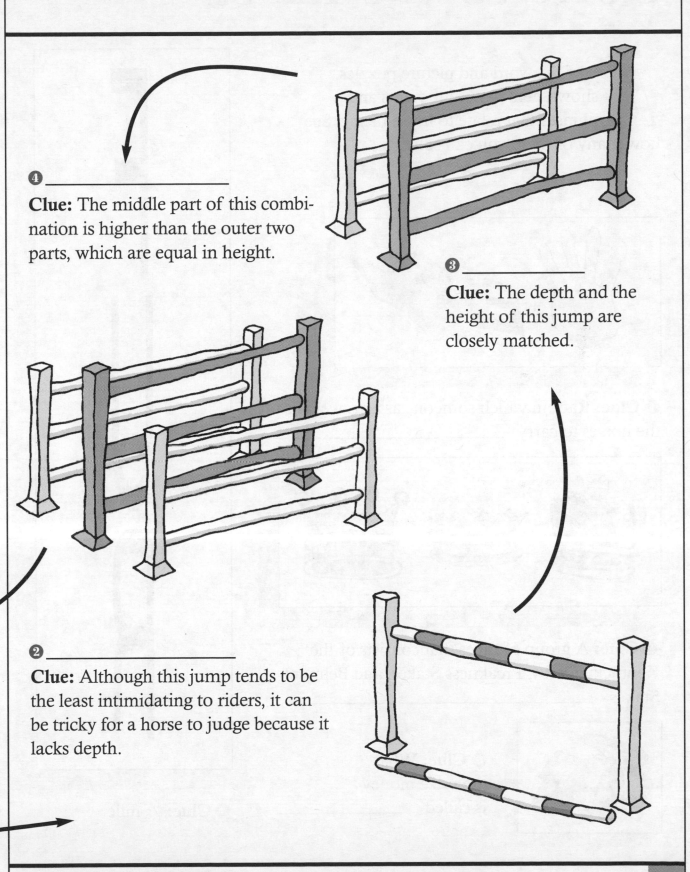

④ _____

Clue: The middle part of this combination is higher than the outer two parts, which are equal in height.

③ _____

Clue: The depth and the height of this jump are closely matched.

② _____

Clue: Although this jump tends to be the least intimidating to riders, it can be tricky for a horse to judge because it lacks depth.

For answers, see page 119

Gone to the Races

All of the word and picture puzzles shown here represent events and phrases that relate to horse racing. See how many of them you can solve.

❶ Clue: Race in which someone assigns weights for the horses to carry _____

❷ Clue: A group of races that consists of the Kentucky Derby, Preakness Stakes, and Belmont Stakes _____

❸ Clue: What the prize money is called _____

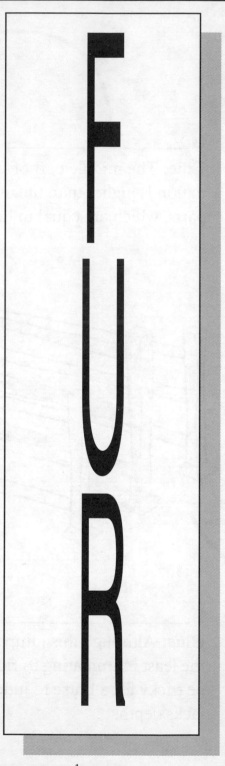

❹ Clue: ⅛ mile

For answers, see page 119

Breeders'

5 Clue: The owners of the horses in this race must pay a nomination fee during the foal's first year

_____

DAILY
DAILY

6 Clue: A bet that involves two races

_____

+ +s

7 Clue: A race in which the winners or a group of winners receive all of the money wagered

_____

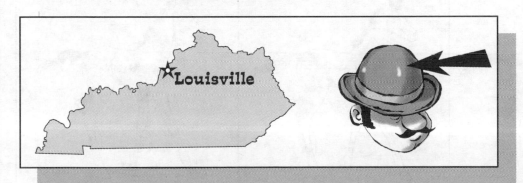

★Louisville

8 Clue: A race that is also known as the Run for the Roses

_____

_____

HOME

9 Clue: The straightaway of the racetrack leading right up to the finish line _____

For answers, see page 119

Pair Up the Pintos

Two of the nine Pinto colts below have identical coat markings. Can you figure out which ones?

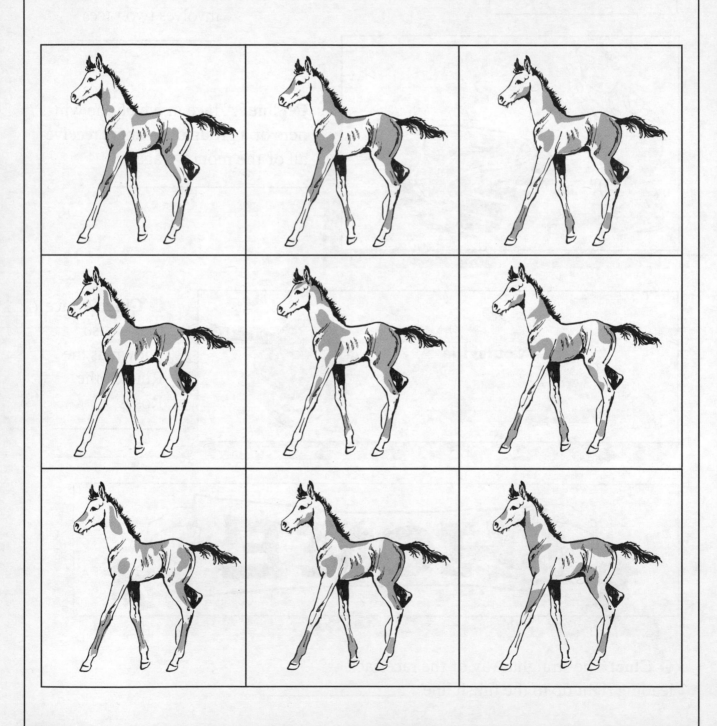

For answers, see page 120

Cowboy Lingo

owdy, pardner! Cowboys share a vocabulary of their very own. See if you can pair each of the terms on the left with the correct definition on the right.

sombrero	to dance
chuck	spurs
dinero	a mustache
amigo	a farmer
boot-scoot	the camp cook
cookie	a friend
dogie	a hat
sodbuster	wages, money
hooks	an orphan calf
cookie duster	food

Country Cowboys

Can you match the following terms for cowhands with the different countries where they are used?

cowhands	Australia
vaqueros	France
stockmen	Mexico
gauchos	United States
guardians	Peru and Chile

For answers, see page 120

Gymkhana Games

During gymkhana competitions, not only do Western riders have to ride as fast as they can, but they need to remember the course for each game as well! See if you can draw the correct riding patterns for the events pictured here.

Keyhole Race

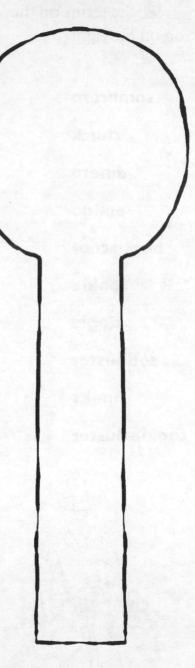

Barrel Race

_____
Start/Finish Line

_____
Start/Finish Line

For answers, see page 120

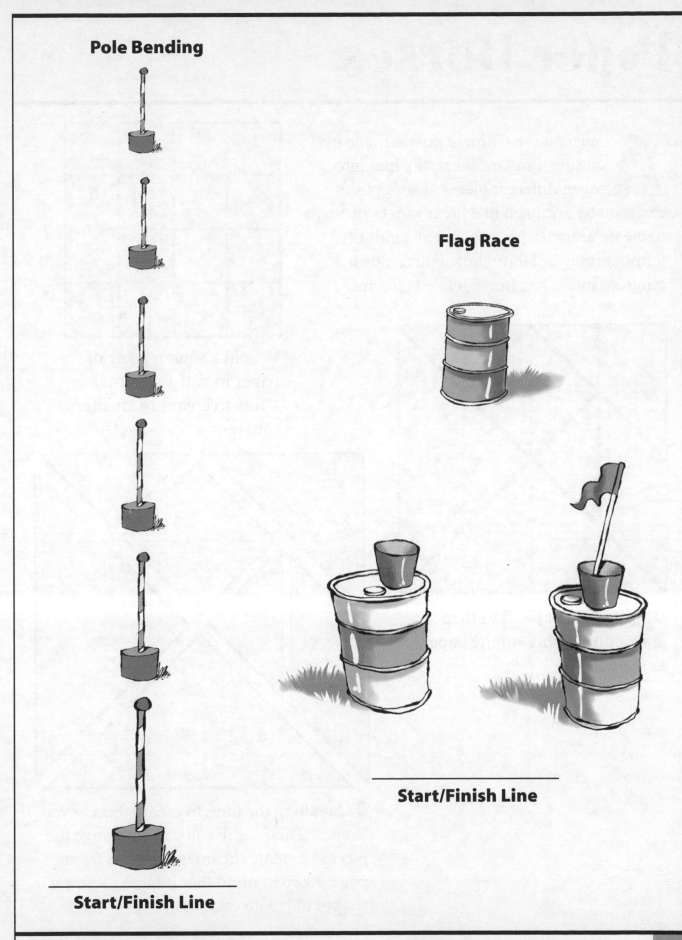

Pole Bending

Flag Race

Start/Finish Line

Start/Finish Line

For answers, see page 120

Paper Horses

A *tangram* is a Chinese puzzle made by cutting a square sheet of paper into seven different pieces. Those pieces can then be arranged in a great variety of ways to create animals, people, and all kinds of familiar images. Here's how you can turn a tangram into a few horse-related pictures.

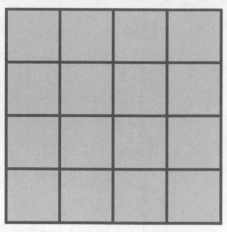

❶ Fold a square piece of paper in half four times in a row to create 16 smaller squares.

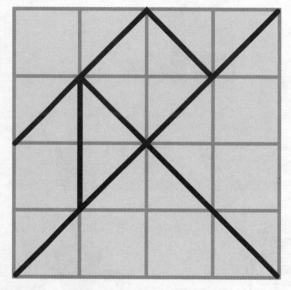

❷ Spread the paper flat, then draw cutting lines on the paper, as shown.

❸ Cut along the lines to create these seven shapes. Then see if you can rearrange the pieces to create the images on the facing page. Keep in mind that it takes all seven shapes to create each image.

For answers, see page 121

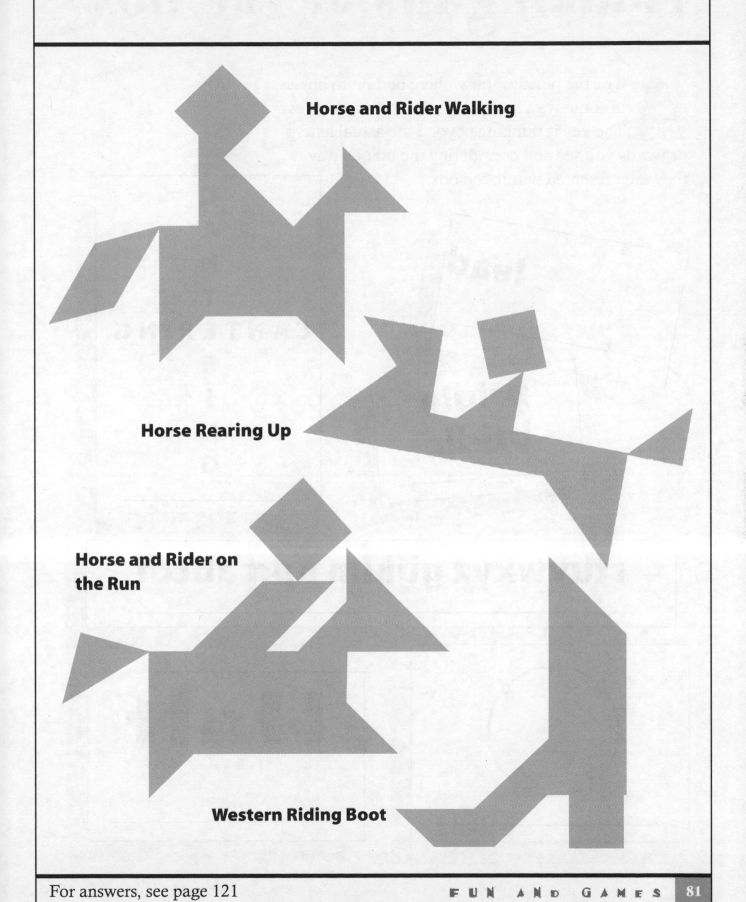

Horse and Rider Walking

Horse Rearing Up

Horse and Rider on the Run

Western Riding Boot

FUN AND GAMES

Thinking Inside the Box

All of the puzzles shown here pertain to horses in some way, but solving them is no easy feat. The key is thinking beyond the actual letters or words you see and considering the unique way they are presented within the box.

lead
_____

bridle
bridle
_____

C
A
N
T
CANTERING
R
I
N
G
_____

rtuvwxyz gijklm npq abcdf
_____

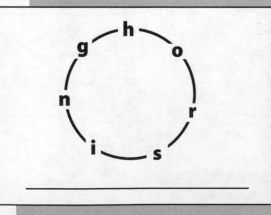

h
g   o
n   r
i   s
_____

Halt
_____

For answers, see page 121

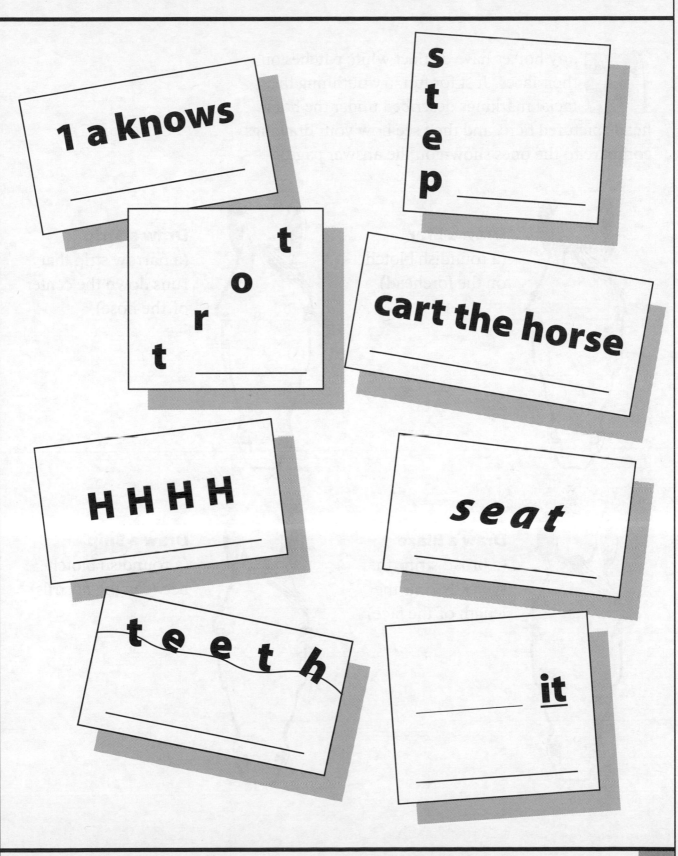

1 a knows
___

s
t
e
p
___

t
r o t
t
___

cart the horse
___

HHHH
___

seat
___

teeth
___

___ it
___

For answers, see page 121

Making Faces

Many horses have distinct white patches on their faces. Just for fun, try outlining the facial markings described under the horse heads pictured here, and then see how your drawings compare to the ones shown on the answer page.

Draw a Star
(a roundish blotch on the forehead)

Draw a Strip
(a narrow strip that runs down the center of the nose)

Draw a Blaze
(a broad stripe that typically runs the length of the face)

Draw a Snip
(a roundish blotch between the nostrils)

For answers, see page 122

Putting On Socks

Horses can have a variety of distinguishable leg markings, too. Try your hand at drawing on the patterns identified below. Put one sock on each leg.

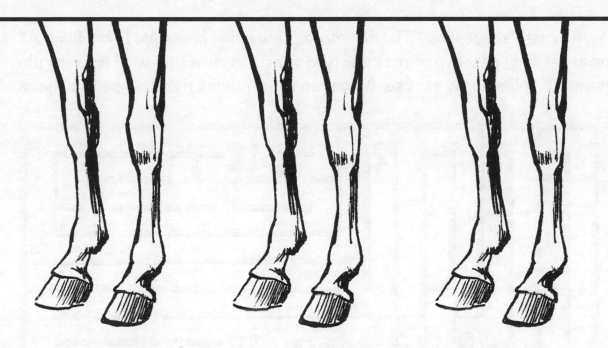

Draw a Coronet Marking
(a thin white band just above the hoof)

Draw a Pastern Marking
(a thick white band that extends from the hoof to just below the fetlock)

Draw a Sock
(a white marking that extends from the hoof to a third of the way up the cannon bone)

Draw a Half-stocking
(white coloring that extends from the hoof to half way up the cannon bone)

Draw a Full Stocking
(white coloring that extends from the hoof to just below the knee)

Draw a Heel Marking
(a blotch of white just above the back of the hoof)

For answers, see page 122

Back to the Barn

You've been riding for about an hour when you realize that you need to be back at the barn in 45 minutes.

"Come on!" says your friend, as she turns off the trail you're familiar with. "I know a shortcut."

"How do you know which way to go?" you ask.

"It's easy," she replies. "The trail markers are riding boots and horseshoes. As long as we don't pass two of the same type of markers in a row, we'll be going the right way." Following her tip, see if you can figure out the right trail back to the barn.

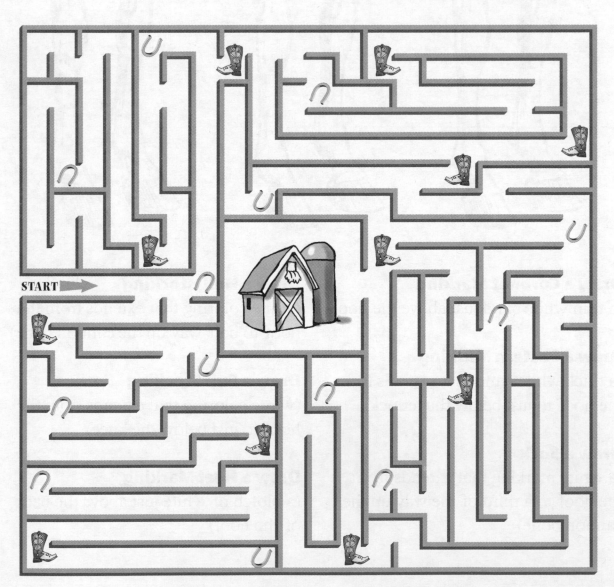

START →

For answers, see page 122

Brain-teasers

Telling Teeth

"**Y**ou can tell how old a horse is by seeing how worn down its teeth are," explained the veterinarian to his new assistant, as he peered into the mouth of a gelding named Dex.

"So, how old is Dex?" asked the assistant.

"Well," responded the veterinarian, "I'd say that in 2 years, Dex will be twice as old as he was 5 years ago!"

Based on what the veterinarian said, can you figure out how old Dex is now?

answer: twelve years old

Secret Cure

What did the veterinarian prescribe when the Palomino came down with a cold?

answer: cough stirrup

Snail's Pace Race

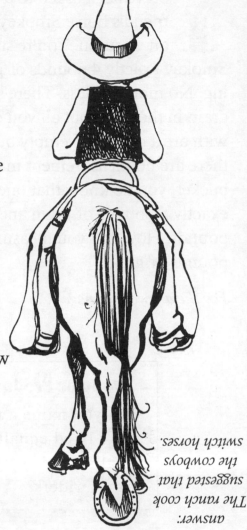

Ever since Roy and Dale signed on at the Friendly Dude Ranch, the two cowboys have been in constant competition. For their next day off, they've planned a race to the river to decide who has the better horse. Frank, the foreman, who's had just about enough of the cowboys' bickering, decides to teach them a lesson.

"Okay," says Frank, "you can race, but the one whose horse takes longer to reach the river wins!"

Not wanting to turn down a challenge, Roy and Dale agree, but since neither one wants to cross the finish line first, they spend the whole day aimlessly wandering around in circles to avoid it.

Long after dinner time, the cowboys, no closer to the river than when they started, cross paths and admit they're tired of this contest but don't know how to end it. The ranch cook just happens to be passing by and offers them a solution. Within seconds Roy and Dale are racing as fast as they can to the river. What did the cook say?

answer: The ranch cook suggested that the cowboys switch horses.

Legs to Stand On

What has six legs, but only four of them touch the ground?

answer: a horse and its rider

Feed Buckets

You've been asked to take care of your friend's horse Smokey while she's away on vacation. You're supposed to feed Smokey exactly 4 pounds of grain at each feeding. No more, no less. There's a whole bin full of grain in the barn, but all you can find to scoop it with are a couple of empty buckets. Although there are no measurement marks on either bucket, you do know that one of them holds exactly 5 pounds of grain and the other exactly 3 pounds. How can you measure out precisely 4 pounds of grain?

For the answer, see page 123

holds exactly 5 pounds of grain

holds exactly 3 pounds of grain

Popular Produce

Can you name a fruit that's liked equally by English and Western riders?

answer: cantelope

Costly Carrots

A Palomino paying for a bag of carrots at the supermarket checkout was short 25 cents. What did he ask the Appaloosa in line behind him?

answer: Can you spot me a quarter?

Horse 'em Foursome

Two fathers and two sons decided to go horseback riding at the Blazing Trails Riding Stable. When they arrived at the stable, there were only three horses available. Just the same, everyone was able to go on a trail ride together, each person riding a different horse.

How was that possible?

For the answer, see page 123

Along for the Ride

A group of equestrians were riding their horses cross-country. One horse was in front of two horses, one horse was behind two horses, and one horse was between two horses.

How many horses were there?

For the answer, see page 123

Horses for Sale

A horse breeder had eight yearlings and sold all but five. How many yearlings did she have left?

answer: five

Another Day

Four Fjord Ponies are named after days of the week that begin with the letter *T*, yet no two of the names are the same.

How can that be?

For the answer, see page 123

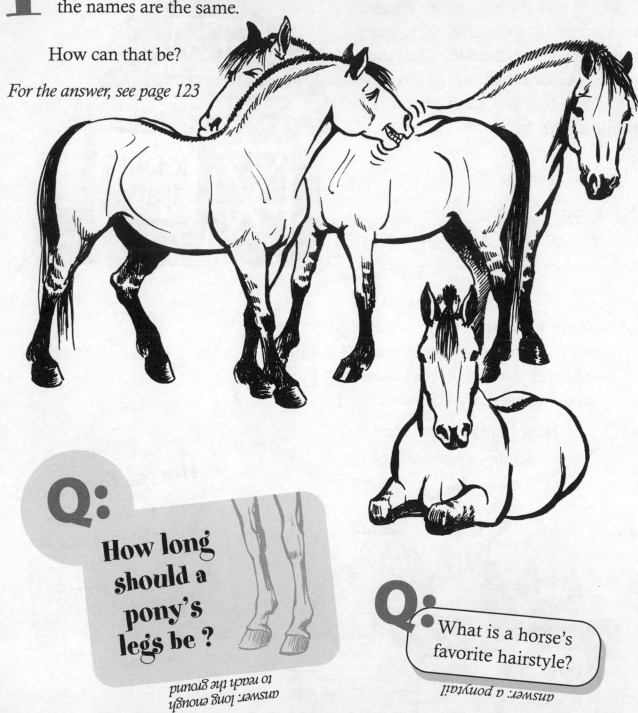

For the answer, see page 123

Q: **How long should a pony's legs be?**

answer: long enough to reach the ground

Q: What is a horse's favorite hairstyle?

answer: a ponytail

The Grain Barrel Mix-Up

In the feed room there are three grain barrels. You can't see what's in them, but they're labeled CORN, OATS, and CORN & OATS, respectively. You just found out that, by mistake, the new stable hand forgot to check the labels and all of the barrels are filled with the wrong types of grain.

Your challenge is to figure out the correct labeling for all three barrels. Here's the hitch: You can look inside only one of them. Which barrel should you open to be able to figure out how all of the barrels should be relabeled, and why?

For the answer, see page 123

Q: What does it take to become a grain train engineer?

answer: plenty of training

Case of the Missing Halter

Blaze's owner can't remember whether she left his new halter in his stall, in the horse trailer, in the tack room, or hanging from one of the fence posts. If only one of the following statements is correct, where is Blaze's halter?

1. The halter is in Blaze's stall.
2. The halter is in the horse trailer or in the tack room.
3. The halter is in Blaze's stall or hanging from one of the fence posts.
4. The halter is not in the horse trailer.

For the answer, see page 123

An Appetizing Apple

Rosie the Roan is clipped to a 10-foot long lead line. Thirty feet across the barnyard, on top of a fence post, is an apple. For some reason, Rosie is able to reach it. Why?

For the answer, see page 123

Where's the Hoof Pick?

Every time the groom misplaces the hoof pick, he finds it in the very last spot he looks. Why?

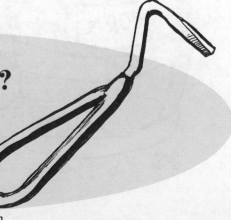

answer: because once he finds it, he quits looking

Lucky Numbers

When they arrive at the horse show, the five contestants from Good Sports Riding Stable think it might bring good luck if they all wore riders numbers that have something in common. At the registration booth, they are told there are only six numbers left to choose from: 2, 3, 7, 10, 11, and 12. After thinking about it for a moment, they decide to take numbers 3, 7, 10, 11, and 12. Why?

Need a hint? Try writing the numbers out as words instead of digits.

For the answer, see page 124

Horse Play

What is a horse's favorite sport?

answer: stable tennis

A Leading Question

If there are five horses in the pasture and you lead one into the barn, how many do you have?

answer: the one you're leading

Flying Along

Two riders live 10 miles apart. They plan to meet up midway between their horse barns. They mount up at exactly the same time and maintain a steady trotting speed of 5 miles per hour. The instant they set out, a horsefly resting on one of the horse's ears starts flying toward the other horse at 15 miles per hour. As soon as it reaches the second horse, it flies back to the first and so on, never changing its speed, until the two riders meet. All in all, how far will the horsefly fly?

For the answer, see page 124

Q:

How do you describe a horse that's standing out in the rain?

answer: under the weather

Daily Doze

Name a horse that never comes out in the daytime.

answer: Pegasus (the constellation)

Crack the Code

The members of the Silver Spurs Riding Club have a special group event planned. At a recent meeting, the club president announced that whoever is first to decode a hidden message in the following list of horse names will have the honor of leading the event. In order to spell out the message, you need to choose one letter from each name in the order they appear. Can you figure it out? Here's a hint: The message reveals what the event is and when it starts. A few letters are already circled to help you get started. *For the answer, see page 124*

MIDNIGH(T), DUCHESS, HON(E)Y, FROSTY, G(E)RONIMO, APPLEJACK,   DAISY, BLUE, JASPER, M(I)SSY, (D)ANCER, PIRATE, BUD, RENEGADE, (G)IZMO, CHIP, PRANCER, HOT-SHOT, ST(A)R, TEX, BA(N)DIT, CISCO, CLEO, WE(N)DY

T _ E   _ R _ _ _   _ I D _   _ _ G _ _ _   A _   N _ _ N

Tools of the Trade

Name an item a horse groom uses that works only when it is full, yet it is always full of holes.

answer: a sponge

Three Little Foals

Ruby's mother had three foals. The first was named Shadow. The second was named Digger. What was the third one called?

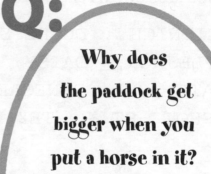

answer: Ruby

Spelled Out

All of a sudden, in the middle of his performance, Tex the Trick Horse stopped and pawed the letters

H I J K L M N O

in the dirt. "Oh," the horse's trainer explained to the audience, "Tex wants a drink of water." How did he know?

For the answer, see page 124

Q:

Why does the paddock get bigger when you put a horse in it?

answer: because it contains more feet

Juggling Carrots

When Jim and Julie finished their riding lesson, their instructor, Ms. Equitation, invited them to help her give treats to all of the horses at the stable. She gave both students an equal number of carrots, the sum of which was the same as the total number of horses. She asked Jim to feed the horses in the west paddock while Julie fed those in the east paddock.

As the two headed toward their respective destinations, Ms. Equitation suddenly called out, "Wait! I forgot that I moved some horses around this morning. There are six more horses in the east paddock than in the west paddock."

How many carrots should Jim give to Julie so that they both have the proper number to feed the horses in their assigned paddocks? *For the answer, see page 124*

Comic Cooldown

What did the groom say when he came to unclip the Thoroughbred from the automatic hot walker?

answer: It's time to stop horsing around

Counting Colts

Two horse breeders met up at the local feed store.

"Say, I heard a few new colts were born at your place this spring," the first one remarked to the other. "What do they look like?"

"Well," answered the second breeder, "they are all buckskins but two, all chestnuts but two, and all roans but two."

How many new foals did the second breeder have altogether?

answer: one buckskin, one chestnut, and one roan

Q: What runs around the barn but stays still?

answer: a fence

Paced to Place

You are a driver in a sulky race. Right before you cross the finish line, you overtake the second-place sulky driver. What position do you finish in?

answer: second, because you overtook the second-place driver

All the Answers

Hungry as a Horse (page 2)

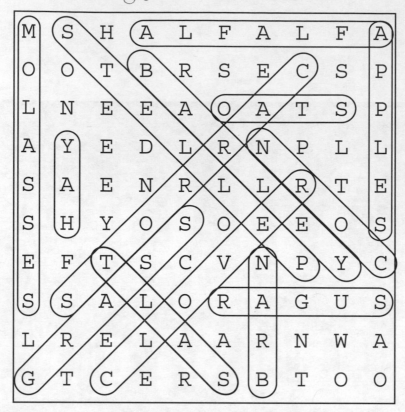

Leftover letters spell:

<u>HORSES</u> <u>NEED</u> <u>PLENTY</u> <u>OF</u> <u>CLEAN</u> <u>WATER</u> <u>TOO</u>!

Horse Stages (page 3)

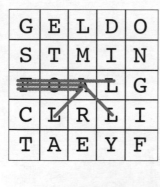

Round Up the Herd (page 4)

- PINTO
- MORGAN
- ARABIAN
- FJORD
- PALOMINO
- CLYDESDALE
- PAINT
- WELSH PONY
- APPALOOSA
- SADDLEBRED
- LIPIZZAN
- THOROUGHBRED
- SHETLAND PONY
- QUARTER HORSE
- TENNESSEE WALKING HORSE

Circle Round (page 5)

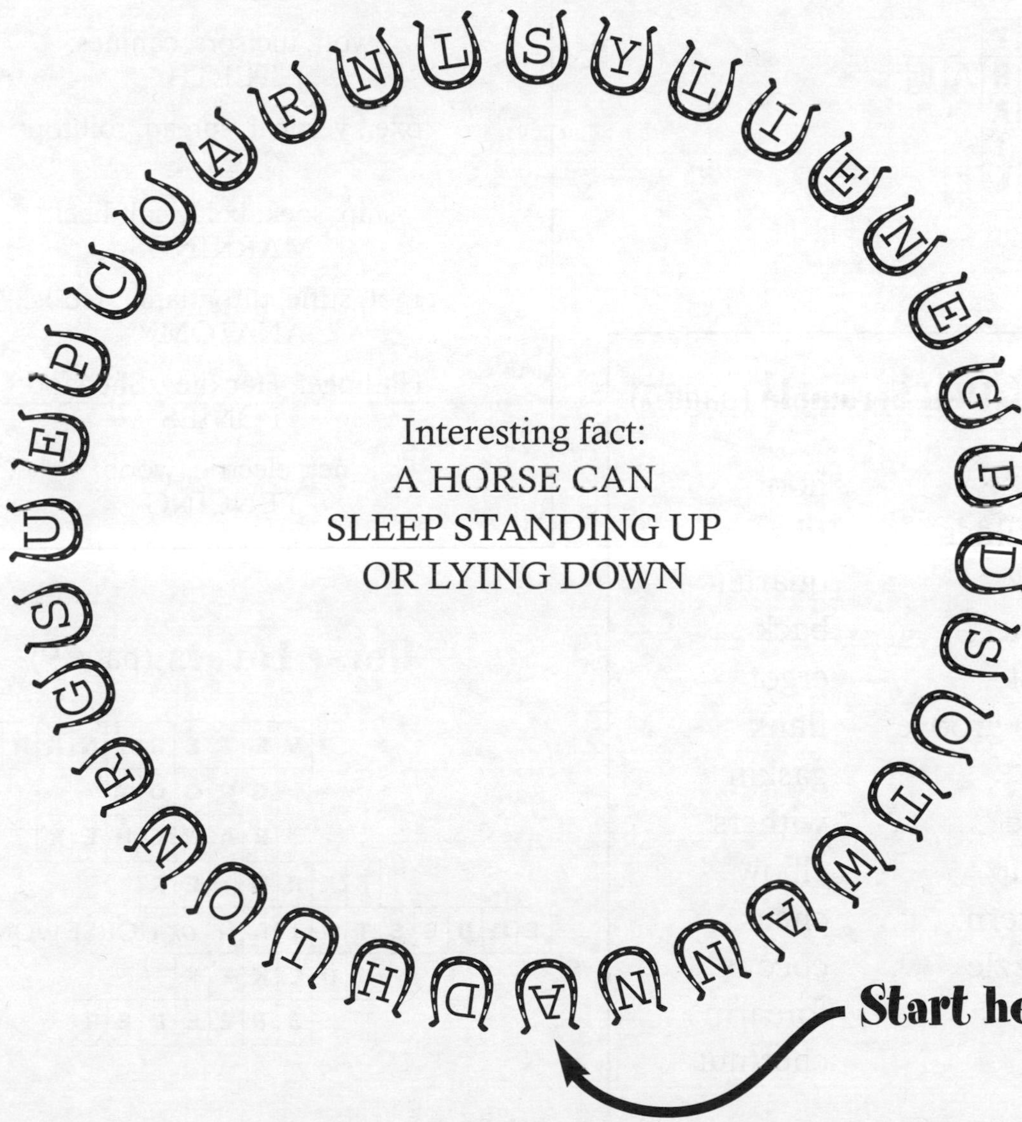

Interesting fact:
A HORSE CAN
SLEEP STANDING UP
OR LYING DOWN

Start here

Horse Sightings (page 6)

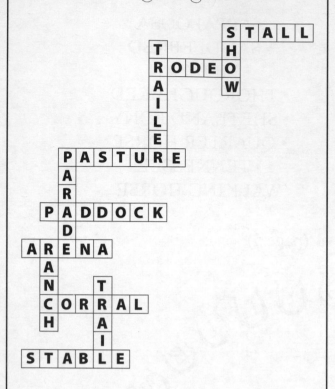

```
                    S T A L L
            T     S H
          R O D E O
          A       O
          I       W
          L
          E
    P A S T U R E
    A
    R
  P A D D O C K
  A   D
A R E N A     T
A   C         R
N O R R A L   A
C             I
H             L
S T A B L E
```

Categories (page 8)

Morgan, Thoroughbred, Arabian, Mustang:
BREEDS

saddle, bridle, martingale, halter, harness:
TACK

stalls, loft, tack room, office:
STABLE

corn, pellets, barley, bran:
FEEDS

snaffle, curb, Pelham, straight:
BITS

cow hocks, parrot mouth, bandy legs, mutton withers:
DEFECTS

wolf, incisors, canines:
TEETH

oxer, vertical, spread, roll top:
JUMPS

snip, sock, bald, half-heel:
MARKINGS

ergot, stifle, throatlatch, fetlock:
ANATOMY

Haflinger, Hackney, Shetland:
PONIES

net, electric, wood:
FENCING

Alphabetical Scramble (page 7)

tail	hoof
shoulder	ribs
dock	quarter
mane	back
crest	ergot
chin groove	flank
jaw	gaskin
stifle	withers
croup	elbow
pastern	cheek
muzzle	coccyx
poll	forearm
eye	chestnut

Horse Lovers (page 9)

```
        V E T E R I N A R I A N
        G R O O M
        R A N C H E R
    F A R R I E R
E Q U E S T R I A N  or HORSEWOMAN
    J O C K E Y
        B R E E D E R
```

In a Name
(pages 10–11)

1. Freddy
2. Priscilla
3. Paul
4. Connie
5. Shirley
6. Theodore
7. Mary
8. Billy
9. Adrienne
10. Andrew

Sidestep (page 13)

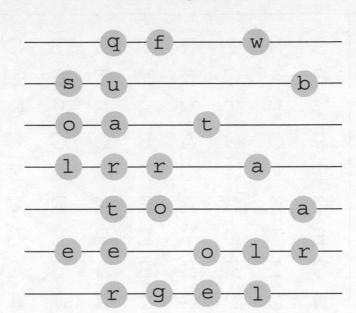

2-in-1 Words (page 12)

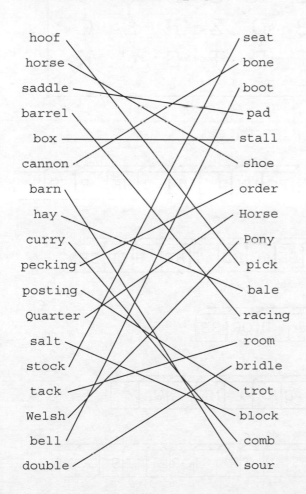

FOOD FOR THOUGHT
(page 14)

Li**pizza**n

d**apple gray**

cribbing

currycomb

limestone

fl**oat**

strawberry roan

egg-bar shoe

liver chestnut

dres**sage**

Pel**ham** bit

Dressing for the Occasion (page 15)

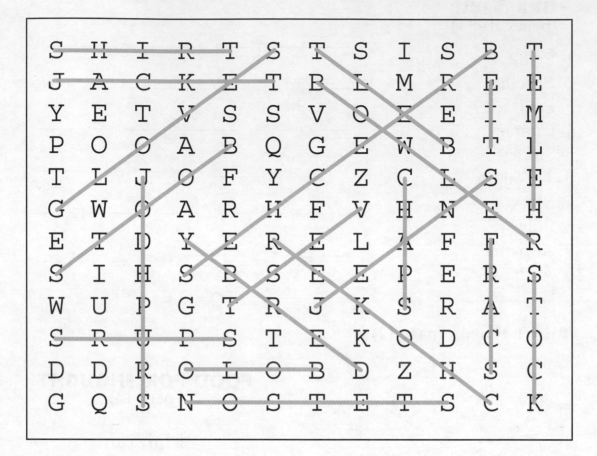

```
S H I R T S T S I S B T
J A C K E T B L M R E E
Y E T V S S V O Z E I M
P O O A B Q G E W B T L
T L J O F Y C Z C L S E
G W O A R H F V H N E H
E T D Y E R E L A F F R
S I H S B S E E P E R S
W U P G T R J K S R A T
S R U P S T E K O D C O
D D R O L O B D Z N S C
G Q S N O S T E T S C K
```

Sugar Cube Sayings (pages 16–17)

1. STRONG AS A HORSE

2. ROUND UP THE HERD

3. PUTTING THE CART BEFORE THE HORSE

4. HUNGRY AS A HORSE

5. WILD HORSES COULDN'T DRAG ME AWAY

6. SHUTTING THE BARN DOOR AFTER THE HORSE IS GONE

A Sweep through the Barn (page 18)

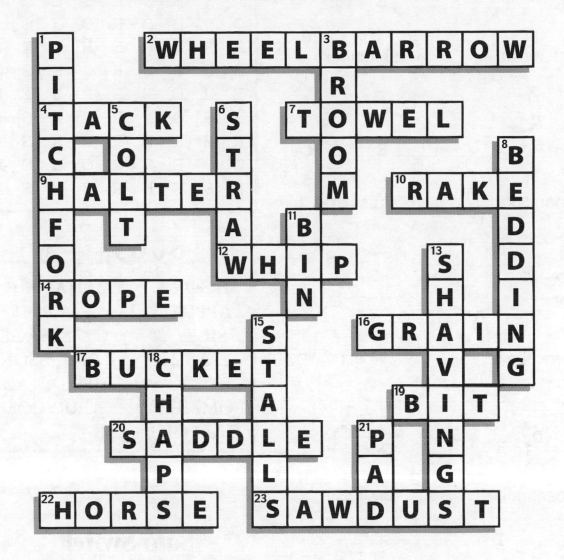

Wacky Phrase Craze (page 19)

1 silly filly
2 gray hay
3 snail trail
4 idle bridle

5 phony pony
6 bad pad
7 coal foal
8 grain train

Riding Rings (pages 20–21)

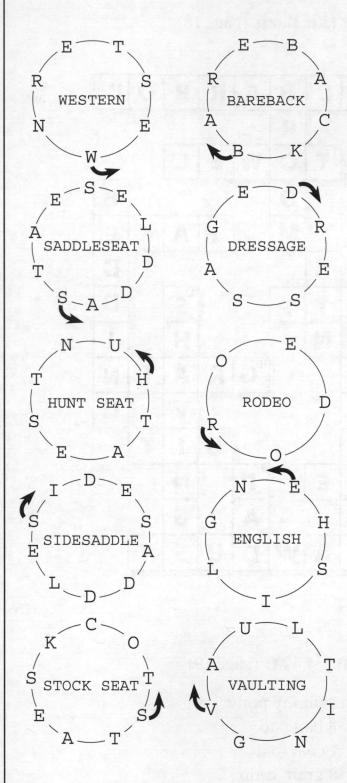

WESTERN

BAREBACK

SADDLESEAT

DRESSAGE

HUNT SEAT

RODEO

SIDESADDLE

ENGLISH

STOCK SEAT

VAULTING

How Many Horses? (page 22)

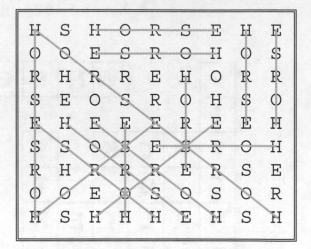

DUOS (page 23)

HOOF	SNAFFLE
APPLE	FARRIER
FILLY	DRESSAGE
LASSO	CAVESSON
STALL	HEADSTALL
POMMEL	CURRYCOMB
GALLOP	

Solo Switch (page 23)

1. FLANK
2. CREST
3. DOCK
4. HOOF
5. LOINS
6. MANE
7. MUZZLE
8. HEEL
9. BACK
10. TAIL

Lead or Trail (page 24)

What is a piebald?

A HORSE THAT IS
BLACK AND WHITE

What is a skewbald?

A HORSE THAT IS WHITE AND
ANY OTHER COLOR
THAN BLACK

Tack Cubes (page 25)

1

h	s	r	f
o	e	e	o
r	a	i	r
n	t	n	k

2

b	s	g	s	c
o	h	i	k	i
s	a	r	i	n
a	n	t	r	c
l	k	h	t	h

3

c	f	p	p	k	l
a	e	o	e	e	i
n	n	m	l	e	n
t	d	m	h	p	i
l	e	e	a	e	n
e	r	l	m	r	g

4

s	b	s	l	t	b	b
n	l	t	e	i	u	r
a	a	i	a	e	c	i
f	n	r	t	d	k	d
f	k	r	h	o	l	o
l	e	u	e	w	e	o
e	t	p	r	n	s	n

Post and Rails (pages 26–27)

CRO**P** · **A**LFALFA · **PA**D · **D**RESSAGE · LASS**O** · **C**ANTER · DOC**K**
(PADDOCK)

FROG · ARENA · CLOVER · BLAZE · **FA**RRIER · RODEO · IRONS · ROACH
(FARRIER)

CORONE**T** · **R**IBBONS · POL**O** · **T**ACK
(TROT)

SADDLE · BI**T** · **A**PPLE · CO**B** · **L**EAD · MAN**E**
(STABLE)

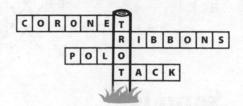

HALTER · PINT**O** · **R**OAN · REIN**S** · **E**RGOT · GROO**M** · **A**RABIAN · MORGA**N** · **S**TALL · CINC**H** · **I**CELANDIC · STIRRU**P**
(HORSEMANSHIP)

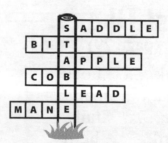

Shadow Boxes (page 28)

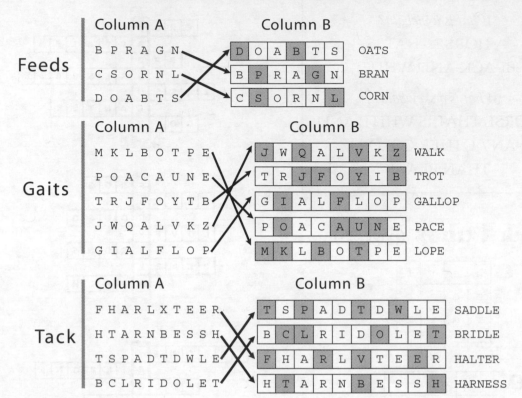

Feeds

Column A

B P R A G N
C S O R N L
D O A B T S

Column B

D O A B T S   OATS
B P R A G N   BRAN
C S O R N L   CORN

Gaits

Column A

M K L B O T P E
P O A C A U N E
T R J F O Y T B
J W Q A L V K Z
G I A L F L O P

Column B

J W Q A L V K Z   WALK
T R J F O Y I B   TROT
G I A L F L O P   GALLOP
P O A C A U N E   PACE
M K L B O T P E   LOPE

Tack

Column A

F H A R L X T E E R
H T A R N B E S S H
T S P A D T D W L E
B C L R I D O L E T

Column B

T S P A D T D W L E   SADDLE
B C L R I D O L E T   BRIDLE
F H A R L V T E E R   HALTER
H T A R N B E S S H   HARNESS

Sounds Just Like . . .
(page 29)

hawk..........hock
main.........mane
tale............tail
heard..........herd
gate...........gait
pole...........poll
hey............hay

STRIKE OUT (page 29)

One Possible Answer:

collect   colt
football   foal
finally   filly
study   stud
marble   mare

Get a Clue! (pages 30–31)

A Palomino   D stable
B equestrian   E martingale
C conformation   F showmanship

Change of Pace (page 32)

trot walk halt bolt prance

pace canter run

jump rack jog lope

Slimmed-Down Sayings (page 32)

1. Never look a gift horse in the mouth.
2. You can lead a horse to water but you can't make him drink.
3. From the horse's mouth

HORSING AROUND (page 33)

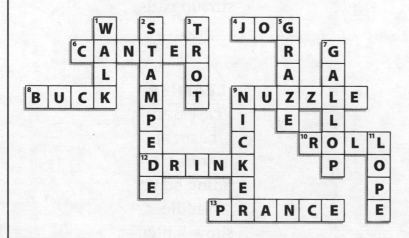

Syllable Shuffle
(pages 34–35)

Draft Horse Breeds
PERCHERON
CLYDESDALE
SHIRE

Pony Breeds
CONNEMARA
HAFLINGER
SHETLAND
WELSH

Pleasure Horse Breeds
ARABIAN
SADDLEBRED
MUSTANG
PAINT

Kinds of Feeds
MOLASSES
BARLEY
BRAN

Types of Grasses
TIMOTHY
CLOVER
RYE

Keeps a Horse Happy and Healthy
INOCULATION
COMPANIONSHIP
EXERCISE
SHELTER
REST

Equine Ailments
CONJUNCTIVITIS
LAMINITIS
FISTULA
STRINGHALT
SPLINTS

Horseshoe Clues (page 36)

Parts of a
B R I D L E ▶

B R O W B A N D
H E A D P I E C E
T H R O A T L A T C H
C H E E K P I E C E S
N O S E B A N D

Parts of a
S A D D L E ▶

S E A T
G I R T H
P O M M E L
C A N T L E
S T I R R U P S
F O R K
H O R N

Another Name (page 37)

1 BOX STALL
2 SEABISCUIT
3 DRAFT HORSE
4 PECKING ORDER
5 RING SOUR
6 SWEAT SCRAPER
7 SALT BLOCK
8 STABLE CLIP
9 SHOWMANSHIP

What's the Deal? (page 38)

METAL
curb
electric fence
horseshoe
lead chain
rasp
shank

RUBBER
bell boots
bit guard
currycomb
grip reins
stall mats
stirrup pads

WOOD
barn
cavelletti
fence post
paddock gate
sawdust
shavings

LEATHER
cavesson
harness
quirt
riding boots
saddle
show halter

Color Codes (page 39)

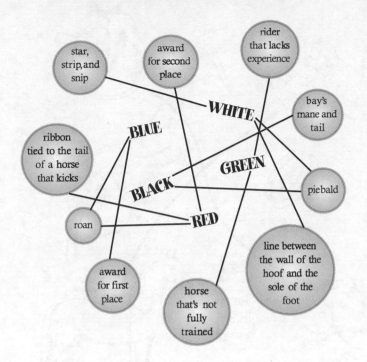

By the Numbers
(page 41)

gallop = 4 beats

pen = 24 by 24 feet

hand = 4 inches

a healthy horse = 99 to 100.5 degrees F

event = 3 riding disciplines

walk = 4 beats

draft horse = 1,500 to 2,200 pounds

lead rope = 8 to 10 feet

canter = 3 beats

box stall = 10 by 12 feet

pony = 14.2 or less hands

trot = 2 beats

Scrambled Solutions (page 40)

1 SEABISCUIT
2 RUG
3 CAN CHASER
4 BLIND SPOTS
5 RIBBONS
6 REIN BACK
7 BAREBACK
8 HEADSHY
9 FAULTS
10 STARGAZER

Desirable Traits (page 42)

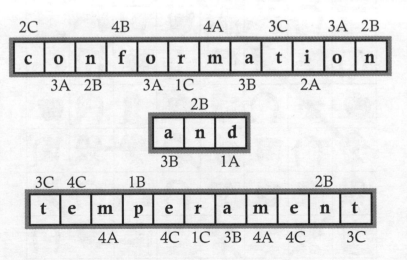

Picture Words
(pages 44–45)

1 horsefly
2 horseshoe
3 sawhorse
4 horseradish
5 horsemanship
6 horsefeathers
7 dark horse
8 horse sense
9 gift horse
10 horse laugh

Double Talk (page 46)

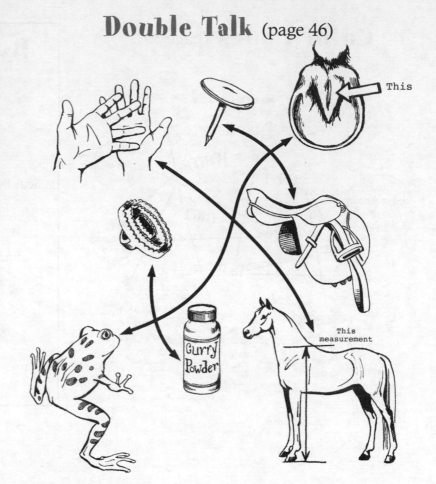

This

This measurement

Curry Powder

Follow the Picture Path (page 47)

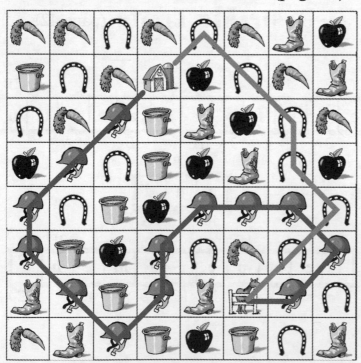

Are You My Type?
(pages 48–49)

Appaloosa
Thoroughbred
five-gaited horse
Tennessee Walking Horse
Icelandic
Grade Horse
Paint
Quarter Horse
Buckskin
Saddlebred

Picture Pairs (pages 50–51)

 **1. piebald**

 **2. tie-down**

 **3. glass eye**

  **4. bell boot**

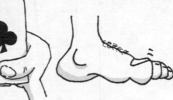 **5. clubfoot**

 6. cannon bone

 **7. quarter crack**

 **8. hay bag**

  **9. neck-rein**

10. salt block

Places & Spaces
(pages 52–53)

❶ paddock

❷ riding ring

❸ box stall

❹ cross-ties

❺ bull pen

❻ hot walker

❼ corral

❽ stable

Animal Menagerie (page 54)

 pigeon-toed

 calf knees

 monkey mouth

 ewe neck

 wolf teeth

 goose rump

 pig eyes

 cow hocks

Horse Sense
(page 55)

1 one-horse town
2 high horse
3 hold your horses
4 horse of a
   different color
5 horseshoes

Tack Up! (pages 56–57)

BRIDLE

SADDLE

1 pair of reins
4 Pelham
5 half moon snaffle
8 egg butt
9 noseband

2 stirrup
3 fork
6 horn
7 cantle
10 skirt

Poisonous Plants (page 58)

1 Henbane
2 Hemlock
3 Fiddleneck
4 Foxglove
5 Buttercup
6 White Snakeroot

In a Word (page 59)

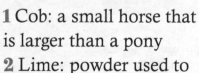

1 Cob: a small horse that is larger than a pony
2 Lime: powder used to keep a stall floor dry
3 Straw: type of bedding
4 Coat: thick layer of hair that covers the horse's body
5 Chestnut: horny patch on the inside of a horse's leg; also a reddish coat coloring
6 Bay: horse with a tan to reddish brown coat and a black mane and tail
7 Crest: curved top line of the horse's neck from the poll to the withers
8 Mash: warm, porridge-like feed usually made with bran
9 Feathers: long hair at the back of the pastern

Motion Pictures (pages 60–61)

 + age = dressage    + trot = foxtrot

 + ter = canter   side + 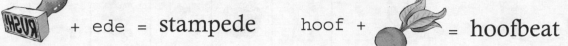 = sidestep

 + ede = stampede   hoof + = hoofbeat

 + gal + = hand gallop   + ing + trot = posting trot

Equine Antics (page 62)

1. roll
2. crib
3. race
4. rear
5. buck
6. whinny
7. prance
8. jump

Rhyme Time (page 63)

 snail/trail   ball/stall

 yarn/barn   paddle/saddle

 bowl/foal   bird/herd

 table/stable    broom/groom

 bolt/colt   sailor/trailer

Picture Spelling Bee (pages 64–65)

broodmare
1. door
2. bear
3. broom
4. bread
5. ram

gelding
1. egg
2. line
3. dig
4. glide
5. lid

stallion
1. ton
2. salt
3. list
4. lion
5. sail

Box Stalls (page 66)

Cooking Up Horse Names
(page 70)

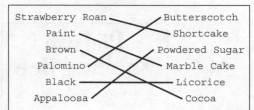

Strawberry Roan — Butterscotch
Paint — Shortcake
Brown — Powdered Sugar
Palomino — Marble Cake
Black — Licorice
Appaloosa — Cocoa

Symbol Squares (page 68)
One Possible Answer:

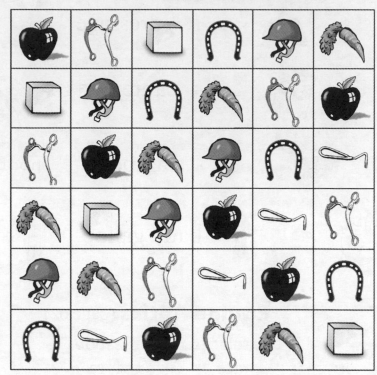

Body Building
(page 69)

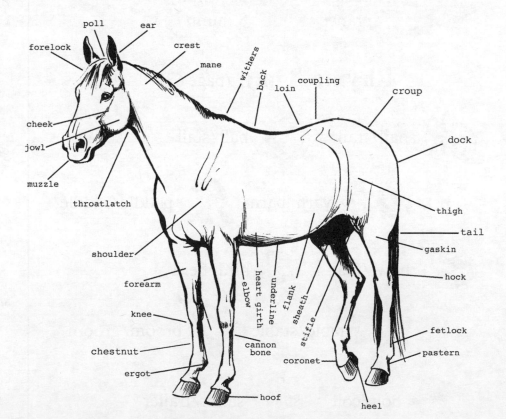

Equine Stall of Fame (page71)

Silver **H**
Brown Beauty **F**
Mr. Ed **L**
The Pie **G**
Duke **B**
Trigger **M**
Buckshot **A**
Poky **C**
Target **E**
Pegasus **K**
Phantom **D**
Buttermilk **I**
Scout **J**

Gone to the Races (pages 74–75)

1 HANDICAP
2 TRIPLE CROWN
3 PURSE
4 FURLONG
5 BREEDERS' CUP
6 DAILY DOUBLE
7 SWEEPSTAKES
8 KENTUCKY DERBY
9 HOMESTRETCH

Stadium Jumping (pages 72-73)

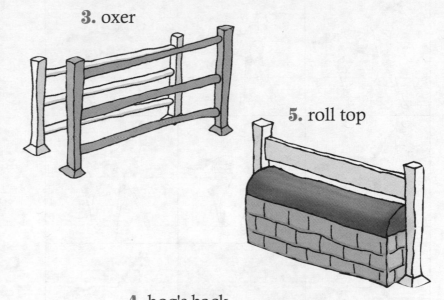
3. oxer

5. roll top

4. hog's back

2. vertical

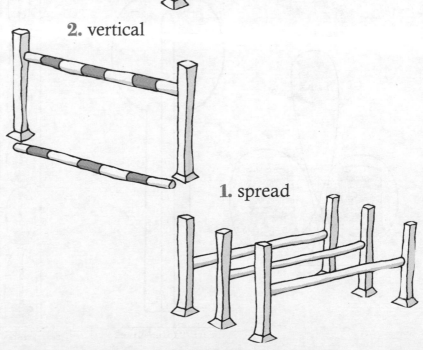
1. spread

Pair Up the Pintos (page 76)

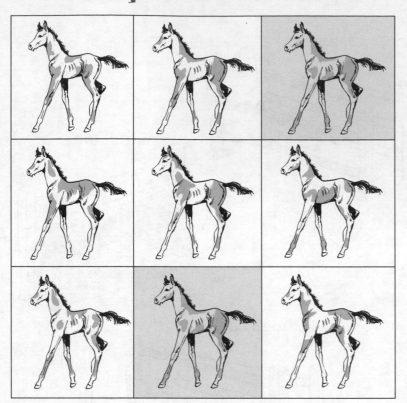

Cowboy Lingo (page 77)

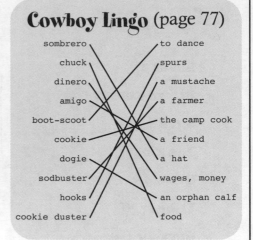

sombrero — a hat
chuck — food
dinero — wages, money
amigo — a friend
boot-scoot — to dance
cookie — the camp cook
dogie — an orphan calf
sodbuster — a farmer
hooks — spurs
cookie duster — a mustache

Country Cowboys (page 77)

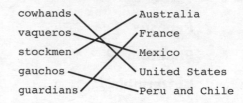

cowhands — United States
vaqueros — Mexico
stockmen — Australia
gauchos — Peru and Chile
guardians — France

Gymkhana Games (pages 78–79)

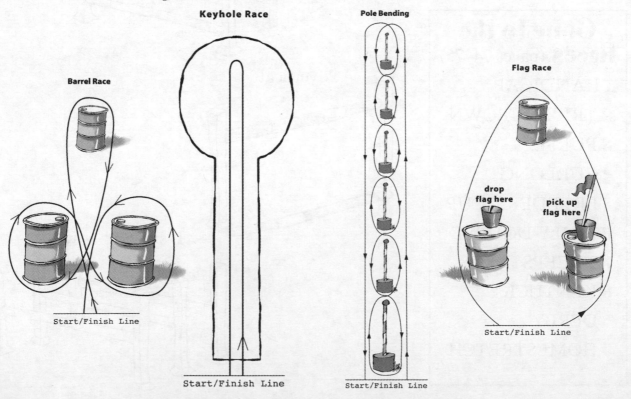

Barrel Race
Start/Finish Line

Keyhole Race
Start/Finish Line

Pole Bending
Start/Finish Line

Flag Race
drop flag here
pick up flag here
Start/Finish Line

Paper Horses
(pages 80–81)

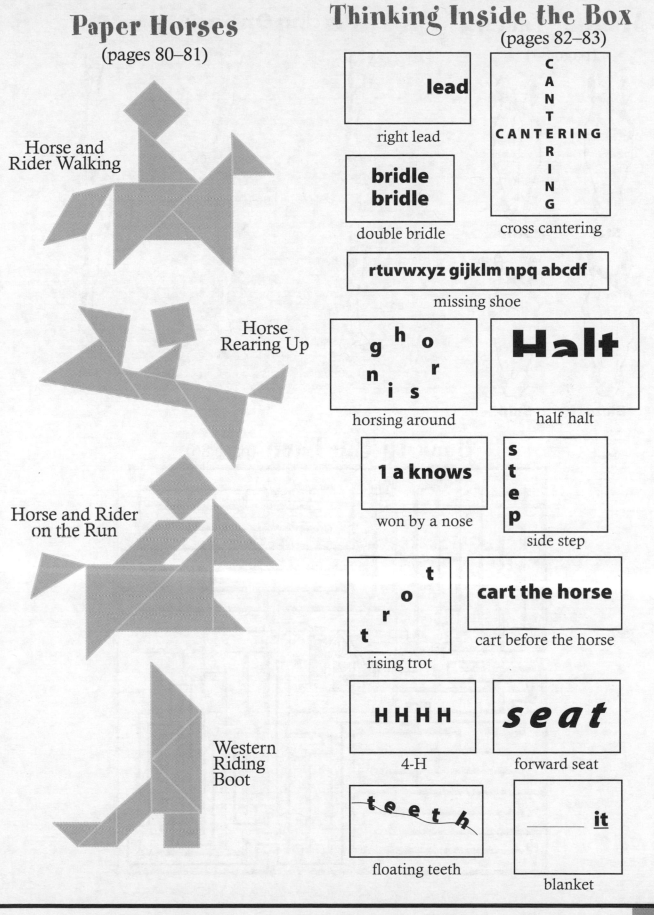

Horse and Rider Walking

Horse Rearing Up

Horse and Rider on the Run

Western Riding Boot

Thinking Inside the Box
(pages 82–83)

lead

right lead

bridle
bridle

double bridle

C
A
N
T
E
R
I
N
G

CANTERING

cross cantering

rtuvwxyz gijklm npq abcdf

missing shoe

g h o
n   r
i s

horsing around

Halt

half halt

1 a knows

won by a nose

s
t
e
p

side step

t
r o
t

rising trot

cart the horse

cart before the horse

H H H H

4-H

seat

forward seat

t e e t h

floating teeth

_____ **it**

blanket

Making Faces
(page 84)

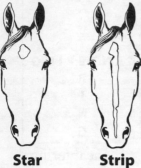

Star

Strip

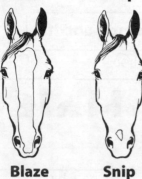

Blaze

Snip

Putting On Socks (page 85)

Coronet Marking

Pastern Marking

Sock

Half-stocking

Full Stocking

Heel Marking

Back to the Barn (page 86)

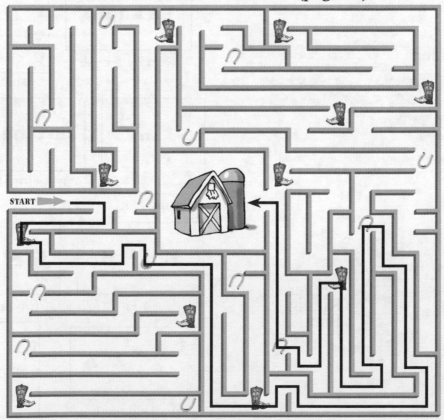

START

Feed Buckets (page 90)

Answer: 1. Fill the 5-pound bucket to the brim, then use it to fill the 3-pound bucket.

2. Dump out the grain in the 3-pound bucket, then pour the 2 pounds left in the larger bucket into the smaller bucket.

3. Refill the 5-pound bucket and pour just enough from it to raise the level in the 3-pound bucket to the brim. This leaves exactly 4 pounds of grain in the 5-pound bucket.

Horse 'em Foursome (page 91)

Answer: The two fathers and two sons were three people altogether: a grandfather, his son, and his son's son.

Along for the Ride (page 91)

Answer: There were three horses traveling in single file.

Another Day (page 92)

Answer: Their names are Tuesday, Thursday, Today, and Tomorrow.

The Grain Barrel Mix-Up (page 93)

Answer: You should look in the barrel labeled Corn & Oats.

Here's Why: Because the barrels are all mislabeled, you know the CORN & OATS barrel is filled with either just corn or just oats. Once you know what is really in it (let's say it's corn), you know what the correct label for the

CORN & OATS barrel should be (CORN).

Next, consider the barrel that's labeled the type of feed that is not in the CORN & OATS barrel (in this case, OATS). There must be either all corn or a mix of corn and oats in that barrel. Well, you already know that the barrel marked CORN & OATS is filled with corn, so the barrel marked OATS must be filled with mixed corn and oats. Through the process of elimination, you know that, in this case, the barrel labeled CORN is filled with oats.

Case of the Missing Halter
(page 94)

Answer: The halter is in the tack room.

Here's Why: If #1 is true, then so is #3. That means that the halter is not in Blaze's stall, nor is it hanging from one of the fence posts, because only one statement can be true. That leaves the horse trailer and the tack room. Now, if the halter is in the horse trailer, statements #2 and #4 would both be true, but remember only one of them can be. That means the halter must be in the tack room.

An Appetizing Apple (page 94)

Answer: The other end of the lead line isn't attached to anything.

Lucky Numbers (page 95)
Answer: When spelled out, numbers 3, 7, 10, 11, and 12 all include the vowel *e*.

Flying Along (page 96)
Answer: Because the riders live 10 miles apart and they are trotting at a rate of 5 miles per hour, they will meet up in exactly 1 hour. Therefore, the horsefly will also fly for a total time of 1 hour. Since it is flying at a rate of 15 miles per hour, it will fly 15 miles in all.

Crack the Code (page 97)
Answer: THE TRAIL RIDE BEGINS AT NOON

Spelled Out (page 98)
Answer: Tex pawed all the letters from H to O (H_2O).

Juggling Carrots (page 99)
Answer: If Jim gives Julie three carrots, Julie will have six more carrots than Jim.

Glossary

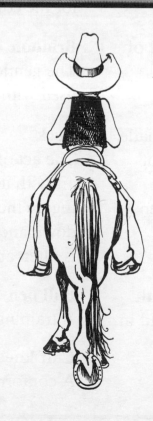

Glossary

Alfalfa
A high-protein hay that is ideally mixed with clover and grass.

Arena
Enclosed area where horses train and compete, usually in Western events such as calf roping.

Barley
A grain that is high in nutrients and gives a horse extra energy. Barley is typically mixed with bran and oats.

Bars of the mouth
The fleshy area between a horse's front and back teeth. This is the part of the mouth where the bit of a bridle fits.

Bell boot
A protective covering, usually made of rubber, that fits over the top of the hoof and protects the horse from injuries. Bell boots are often used on horses that overreach.

Bolo
A string tie worn by Western riders. A bolo tie is commonly held in place with an ornamental clasp.

Bosal
A rawhide noseband that is part of a hackamore bridle used in Western riding. A bosal, which controls the horse by applying pressure on the horse's nose, takes the place of a bit.

Breeches
Comfortable, stretchy riding pants worn by English riders.

Breeders' Cup
A race that requires a horse owner to pay a nomination fee during the foal's first year in order to qualify for the competition.

Bridoon
The gentler of two bits that are used with a double bridle.

Buck
The act of a horse leaping in the air with its back arched and landing on the ground with its head down and its forelegs stiff. Bucking is often an attempt to throw a rider.

Bull pen
A training corral.

Calf knees (back at the knee)
A conformation fault in which the

knees, when viewed from the side, appear hollowed in instead of rounded out. This condition affects the way the horse travels, and strains the legs.

Cannon bone
The long straight bone that extends from the knee to the fetlock on a horse's foreleg and from the hock to the fetlock on the hind leg.

Canter
A smooth, three-beat gait that is faster than a trot and slower than a gallop.

Cantle
The rounded portion that slopes up at the very back of the saddle tree.

Cavesson
The part of a bridle that goes over the horse's nose and under the jaw.

Chaps
Protective leather leg coverings often worn by Western riders.

Chestnut
A horny circular patch on the inside of a horse's leg; a red coloring with red mane and tail.

Choker
A necktie that is worn as part of a rider's formal attire.

Cinch
Western-style girth strap used to hold the saddle in place.

Clubfoot
A hoof with an abnormally short toe and long heel.

Cob
A short-legged horse that is slightly larger than a pony.

Coccyx
The horse's tailbone.

Colt
A young male horse, generally up to the age of four.

Conformation
A horse's physical characteristics judged according to how they compare to the ideal shape and form.

Conjunctivitis
An inflammation of the membrane covering the front of the eyeball and lining the eyelid.

Coronet
The band of soft tissue just above the horse's hoof at the base of the leg.

Corral
The Western term for a relatively small, fenced-in turnout area.

Cow hocks
A conformation flaw in which the hocks are too close together.

Crest
The curved line created by the top of a horse's neck, from the poll to the withers, where the mane grows.

Cribbing
A bad habit in which a horse clamps its teeth onto a solid object, such as a fence, and sucks in air.

Crop
A short riding whip sometimes used to reinforce a rider's leg signals.

Cross cantering
A manner of cantering in which a horse leads with one front foot and the opposite hind foot. Cross cantering is a very uncomfortable gait for the rider.

Cross-ties
A pair of ropes or light chains that extend from sturdy facing walls or posts and clip to the sides of a horse's halter. Cross-ties minimize side-to-side movement, making it safer for grooms, veterinarians, farriers, and other individuals to work on a horse.

Croup
The top of a horse's rump.

Curb
A bit that includes a mouthpiece, shanks, and often a curb strap or chain. These pieces work together to apply leveraged pressure to the horse's jawbone.

Currycomb
A round rubber or plastic grooming tool equipped with short triangular teeth for loosening and removing dirt, hair, and dander from a horse's coat.

Daily double
A horse-racing bet that is based on two races.

Derby (bowler)
A style of hat considered part of the formal attire for Saddle Seat equitation and some other forms of English riding.

Dock
The flesh and bone portion of a horse's tail.

Double bridle
A bridle that includes both a curb bit and a small snaffle bit.

Dressage
A sophisticated style of riding that trains a horse to perform refined maneuvers in response to a rider's body signals.

Egg-bar shoe
An oval horseshoe that provides additional support beneath the horse's heel.

Equestrian
A person who is well versed in riding horses.

Ergot
A horny growth at the rear of the fetlock.

Ewe neck
A thin, weak neck with little or no flexibility at the poll.

Farrier
A person who trims hooves and shoes horses.

Fender
The leather panel on a Western saddle that holds the stirrup and protects the rider's leg.

Fetlock
The round, bony part of a horse's leg just above the pastern.

Filly
A female horse up to the age of four.

Fistula of the withers
A rawness or bruising of the withers that can lead to serious infection.

Flank
The area of a horse's side between the barrel and the thigh.

Floating teeth
The practice of rasping off the sharp points on a horse's teeth.

Foal
A newborn horse.

Fork
The forward part of a saddle tree that fits over the horse's withers.

Forward seat
A style of Hunt-Seat riding in which a rider inclines her upper body forward slightly in all gaits faster than a walk.

Fox-trot
One of the distinctive slow gaits associated with a five-gaited horse.

Frog
A V-shaped portion of the underside of the foot that acts as a shock absorber whenever the hoof strikes the ground.

Furlong
A horse-racing measurement that equals one-eighth of a mile.

Gallop
A four-beat gait by which a horse achieves its greatest speed.

Gaskin
The hind leg muscle located between the hock and the stifle. The gaskin is equivalent to the human calf muscle.

Gelding
A male horse that has been castrated.

Girth
A leather, cotton, or synthetic belly strap to hold an English saddle in place.

Glass eye
The blue eye sometimes seen in an Appaloosa, Paint, or mixed-breed horse.

Goose rump
A conformation fault in which the horse's rump is sharply sloped. A horse with a goose rump may have less than desired strength in the hindquarters.

Grade horse
An unregistered horse.

Half-halt
A signal for the horse to collect itself in preparation for a change in gait, speed, or direction.

Half-moon snaffle
A type of snaffle bit that has an unjointed mouthpiece. The action of this bit is mostly felt at the horse's lips, the corners of the mouth, and the tongue.

Handicap
A horse race in which the competitors are assigned different weight, time, or distance penalties in order to equalize the chance of winning.

Hand
A 4-inch unit of measurement used to determine a horse's height at the withers.

Headshy
A horse that resists having its head, face, or ears touched.

Headstall
The part of a bridle that extends down from the top of the horse's head behind the ears and attaches to the cheekpieces.

Hock
The hind leg joint located between the stifle and the cannon bone. The hock is the horse's hardest-working joint and is equivalent to the human ankle.

Hog's back
A type of jump in which the center fence is the highest and the front and back fences are equal in height.

Homestretch
The straightaway leading to the finish line on a racetrack.

Horsefeathers
An expression often used when a person doesn't believe something he has heard, as would be the case if someone claimed that horses have feathers.

Horse laugh
A loud, rowdy laugh.

Horse sense
Practical, common knowledge.

Hot walker
A rotating machine that is used to lead a hot horse in a circle in order to properly cool down.

Hunt Seat
A basic style of English riding that includes working on the flat and jumping.

Inoculation
An annual vaccination given to a horse to keep it healthy.

Jodhpurs
English riding–style pants made out of stretch fabric to accommodate the movements of the rider.

Jog
Western riding term for a two-beat gait similar to the trot but a bit slower and more easygoing.

Keeper
A small leather loop that holds the end of a bridle strap in place.

Kentucky Derby
One of the most popular annual horse races in the United States. The Kentucky Derby, also called the Run for the Roses, is one of the three races that make up the Triple Crown.

Laminitis
Painful swelling of the inner tissues of the hoof wall, often brought on when a horse that has not been properly cooled down after exercise eats too much grain or drinks too much water.

Lead
The term that refers to the front leg and the opposite hind leg that first strike the ground when a horse canters. When cantering clockwise in a circle, a horse should lead with its right front leg; when cantering counterclockwise, its left front leg.

Limestone
A rock consisting of calcium carbonate that is available in granulated form and is often sprinkled on stall floors to help keep them

Limestone *(cont'd)*
dry and deodorized.

Lope
Western riding term for a smooth three-beat gait similar to the canter but a bit slower.

Mare
A female horse that is more than four years old.

Martingale
A strap used to keep a horse from tossing its head too high. The more restrictive type, a *standing martingale*, threads through a strap that goes around the horse's neck and attaches at one end to the underside of the noseband and at the other end to the girth. The *running martingale,* which is less restrictive, also attaches to the girth but has two straps extending from the neck strap that attach to the reins with metal rings.

Mash
Grain, usually bran, that is moistened with hot water to provide a warm, porridgelike feed for a cold or sick horse.

Monkey mouth
A conformation fault in which a horse has an underbite.

Muzzle
The portion of a horse's face that consists of the nose and lips.

Neck-rein
A way of signaling a horse to turn that is used in Western-style riding. Holding the reins in one hand, the rider signals a right turn by laying the left rein against the horse's neck and a left turn by laying the right rein against the horse's neck. The horse responds by moving away from the rein in the desired direction.

Nuzzling
The act of a horse using its nose to touch, rub, or push something.

Oxer
A jump that combines two fences so that the depth and the height of the obstacle are closely matched.

Pace
A gait, seen mostly in harness racing, in which the front and hind legs of the same side strike the ground at the same time, followed by the opposite front and hind legs striking the ground simultaneously. The pace is usually a little faster than the trot.

Paddock
The English term for a fenced-in turnout area. It can range up to an acre in size.

Pastern
The angled section located between the hoof and the fetlock that acts as a shock absorber for the horse's leg.

Pelham bit
A combination bit that can be used as a snaffle or a curb.

Pellets
Processed feed that contain grains, hay, or both grains and hay and sometimes vitamin and mineral supplements. Pellets are easy to store and to measure.

Pig eyes
Small eyes that may partially limit a horse's scope of vision.

Pigeon-toed
A conformation fault in which a horses' hooves turn in toward each other. Horses that are pigeon-toed are more likely to strain their leg joints.

Poll
A very sensitive spot between the horse's ears where the skull and backbone meet.

Pommel
The front portion of the saddle that fits over the withers.

Posting trot (rising trot)
A trot during which the rider rhythmically rises out of the saddle at every other stride to achieve comfort and maintain control while moving at a brisk pace.

Purse
The prize money awarded at a horse race.

Quarter crack
A crack that can develop in the hoof when the hoof wall becomes too long or dry and brittle.

Rein back
A term for signaling a horse to back up.

Roach
To cut or shave a mane so that it is very short. Western cutting horses often have roached manes to prevent the reins from tangling in them when they work or compete.

Roan
A coat coloring that features a mix of dark and light hairs that create a mottled or speckled look. Blue roans have a mix of white and black hairs; red or strawberry roans have a mix of white and brown or auburn hairs.

Rodeo
A competitive demonstration of Western riding skills that include cutting, roping, bronc and bull riding, and steer wrestling.

Roll top A solid, curved jump that is topped with a rail.

Saddle Seat A style of English riding that was originally developed to highlight the action of the American Saddlebred Horse and has since been adapted to suit Arabians and Morgans.

Shank The part of a curb bit extending below the mouthpiece that the rein attaches to.

Shavings Flaky wood chips that are used as bedding in a horse stall.

Side step (sidepass) When a horse crosses one front foot in front of the other, moving sideways instead of forward.

Skirt A leather flap extending from the side of a saddle.

Snaffle A gentle bit that works by applying direct pressure to the corners of the mouth, the bars, and the lips (rather than the leveraged pressure of a curb bit).

Sole Underside of the hoof located between the white line and the bars and frog.

Splints Bony enlargements of the splint bones, which are located along both sides of the back of the cannon bone.

Spread A jump that combines two to four fences that are set close together.

Spurs An artificial aid made of metal that attaches to a rider's boot. Spurs are properly used to reinforce a rider's leg signals in case the horse does not respond to them.

Stallion A mature male horse (usually more than three to five years old) that has not been gelded.

Stampede The sudden flight of a herd of frightened horses.

Stetson A style of hat popular with Western riders.

Stifle The joint located at the top front of the hind leg.

Stock A narrow white scarf worn around the rider's neck that is part of a formal hunt or show outfit.

Stock seat The basic riding style practiced by Western riders.

Straw Stalks or stems from grain plants used as bedding for a horse's stall.

Stringhalt A nervous disorder that causes a horse to move its hind legs in an exaggerated flexing way when walking.

Sweepstakes A horse race in which the winners receive all of the bet money.

Tack Halters, bridles, saddles, harnesses, and other gear that's used to control horses.

Triple Crown The trio of famous horse races that consists of the Belmont Stakes, the Preakness, and the Kentucky Derby. Few horses have become Triple Crown winners.

Toe The center front portion of the hoof.

Trot A two-beat gait, faster than the walk and slower than the canter, during which the horse's diagonal pair of legs (one front leg and the opposite hind leg) move together.

Vaulting An equine sport in which riders perform gymnastic moves atop the back of a trotting or cantering horse.

Vertical A jump that consists of a single fence.

Wall The outer surface of the hoof.

Withers The elevated top of the horse's shoulders, located at the neck, that helps keep the saddle in place.

Wolf teeth Small teeth located in front of the upper molars that can interfere with the action of the bit.

Yearling A foal that is more than one year old.

Alphabetical List of Games

Draw Your Favorite Horse Here...

Other Storey Books You Will Enjoy

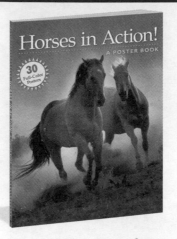

Jessie Haas
This treasure chest of a book has enough info and fun to keep horse-obsessed kids busy for hours. For ages 8 and up, young readers can make crafts for human and equine friends alike and learn all about their favorite horses.

Horses caught in action are exciting to behold, and these 30 thrilling, pull-out posters will delight horse-loving youngsters everywhere.

Illustrations by Lindsay Graham
Full-color backgrounds and reusable vinyl stickers keep children busy creating equine dramas, while the accompanying text teaches them about life on the horse farm.

Cindy A. Littlefield
Using the easy step-by-step instructions and some basic craft supplies, kids ages 8 to 12 can create their own herd of model paper horses.